OPEN-EYED, FULL-THROATED

Nathalie Anderson
editor

OPEN-EYED, FULL-THROATED
An Anthology of American/Irish Poets

ARLEN
HOUSE

Open-Eyed, Full-Throated

is published in 2019 by
ARLEN HOUSE
42 Grange Abbey Road
Baldoyle
Dublin 13
Ireland
Phone: +353 86 8360236
Email: arlenhouse@gmail.com

978–1–85132–212–1, paperback

International distribution by
SYRACUSE UNIVERSITY PRESS
621 Skytop Road, Suite 110
Syracuse, New York
USA 13244–5290
Phone: 315–443–5534/Fax: 315–443–5545
Email: supress@syr.edu
www.syracuseuniversitypress.syr.edu

Typesetting by Arlen House

Front cover artwork: 'The Tourist' by Randall Exon
is reproduced courtesy of the artist

Back cover artwork: 'Ballycastle Beach No. 37' by Logan Grider
is reproduced courtesy of the artist

CONTENTS

INTRODUCTION

The poets gathered in this anthology have come together through our work in Irish Studies, and more particularly through our association with the American Conference for Irish Studies (ACIS), an organization devoted to the study of Irish culture, history, politics, religion, art, music and literature. Since about 2000, the ACIS annual meetings have included readings by scholars who are also poets, members of the organization who use their expertise not only to explore Irish materiality through research and analysis, but also to respond emotionally, conflictedly, ecstatically, ironically, through their art. We have titled these readings – and now this anthology – *Open-Eyed, Full-Throated* to convey the premise that our scholarly work in Irish Studies makes us knowing observers of Irish culture, positioned to perceive complexity and nuance, aware of our own distance from the language and society we study, yet often moved to intensities of speech by what we observe and experience and comprehend.

Many – though not all – of the poets included in this anthology share an Irish heritage. Most reside in the United States, but some were born in Ireland, and some live there currently. While the matter of Ireland engages us – its landscapes, its myths, its literary riches, its vexed colonial past, its recent sectarian Troubles, its sexual repressions, its economic tribulations, its ecological challenges, its increasing cultural diversity – the poetry included here is still more wide-ranging, responding to personal loss, to local dilemmas, to global distress, to unanticipated joy. One of the great pleasures of our readings over these past 20 years is our collective idiosyncrasy, our diverse individuality. We offer the reader forty four voices, distinct and distinctive, but together forming a chorus of focused intensity.

The images on the cover of the anthology seem to us emblematic of this enterprise. Randall Exon and Logan Grider are American artists affiliated with the Ballinglen Art Foundation on the north coast of Mayo.

Exon's 'The Tourist' seems precisely to embody the poet's eagerness, openness, attentiveness and curiosity, while also marking the slight distance, the slight separation, involved in intellectual inquiry.

Grider's sculpture evokes the landscape just visible in Exon's painting, but his artistic method is even more relevant: 'Ballycastle Beach No. 37' is composed from the plastic detritus now washing up daily on Ireland's once-pristine shores.

Creating beauty and significance from the disquieting: this is an impetus the poets in this volume share, a response to the challenges facing all of us in a changing world.

– Nathalie Anderson

Alexander Griswold Cummins Professor of English Literature
and Director of the Program in Creative Writing
Swarthmore College

March 2019

OPEN-EYED, FULL-THROATED

NATHALIE ANDERSON

Nathalie Anderson is an award-winning poet, accomplished librettist, and Alexander Griswold Cummins Professor of English Literature at Swarthmore College, where she directs the Program in Creative Writing. Her books include *Following Fred Astaire, Crawlers, Quiver, Stain*, and the chapbook *Held and Firmly Bound*. She's anthologized in *The Book of Irish American Poetry from the Eighteenth Century to the Present*. Anderson has authored libretti for five operas in collaboration with composer Thomas Whitman. She has served the American Conference for Irish Studies as President of the Southern Regional ACIS and as Arts Representative, and organizes the Open-Eyed, Full-Throated readings for the organization.

CANAL BANK BALK
John Coll's statue of Patrick Kavanagh, Dublin

And pressed at midnight in some public place
Live lips upon a plummet-measured face.
– William Butler Yeats, 'The Statues'

Can't say I really know the man. Can't say what he'd say
to all our invasive intimacies, all our forced
familiarities. I mean, who wouldn't want to rub
shoulders with muchness. Want to rub his shoulders. Rub
his patinated crotch. Take disgraceful photos. I mean,
how smooth the move from a quick touch to a fast grip; how
easily a tap on the bicep slides over to become the arm
slung round the neck, a stranglehold; how fast the friendly
brushing back of hair splays into a palming of the skull,
maybe in blessing, maybe phrenologically assessing?

He brings it on himself, so rumpled he invites straightening,
his legs lazed out, soft collar open. Yeah, somebody's
laid it on thick, like he's been slabbed up out of the clay –
how earthy he is, how available, with his loose shoes,
his daily paper folded thick and jammed in a jacket pocket,
his slouch hat laid by. Yet at the same time he's
so well defended, arms crossed like a closed gate, eyes
unreadable behind his massive glasses. Maybe he's
amused. Maybe he's standoffish. Stoic. Contemplative.
Abstracted. No wonder we want to shake him.

O commemorate me! Where there is water there's
sure to be more water: the sluice gate in spate, showers
pocking the canal's smooth face, wet sparrows flapping,
and you can bet there's been unzipping – the jacking off,
the pissing about. What does he make of all this aberrance?
He could be thinking *an impotent worm on his thigh.*
He could be thinking *hard as a Protestant spire.*
He could be thinking *pleasures that we missed by inches.*

He could be thinking *coughed the prayer phlegm up.*
He could be thinking *a wet sock* or *her own dark hair* or *stilly*

greeny. I've sat that lap. I've kissed those lips. Nothing
disturbs his privity. The line of his mouth, the line
of his slouch, the line of his groin neither rises nor falls.
He sits there imperturbable whatever the liberties, his
big hands, his big ears, always listening but never quite
to you. Oh yes, he suffers fools, offers a seat on the bench
to any passer-by, offers himself as exemplum – his
stillness, his inwardness. Sets down his hat with purpose,
a barrier every one of us ignores. Go on, try him.
Call him by the pet name he still won't answer to.

REUNION

On the very afternoon when the mimosas shifted,
folding in their feathery fans to swag their sleeves in coin,
who should turn up again but Ulysses, fleshier himself
these days, and similarly dripping with gold. Came back

tale-telling, gregarious, as full of himself as ever,
the face, the body thickened with experience but still
approximating unmistakably the man she'd known,
the ring big on his finger, the eyes holding hers. Came back

apologizing for the past however many years when
(always the wily one, always after something) he'd used her
ill, he said. Then back to his tale of mayhem, all of it
certainly diverting – though, from what did he divert her?

On the very afternoon when the cicadas stilled themselves for
whole unsettling minutes while the winds changed their
courses, she stood similarly stunned, caught strangely wrong-
footed, not sure what she should be feeling. How had her story

turned into one of his, the nostalgia so thick on the air
he was near to weeping with it? An invitation
that wouldn't be an invitation. You didn't think I
meant Penelope? Swine and swineherd, pigsty and pig. Like

in all those years she hadn't again and again moved on,
thinking of him, sure, from time to time, but nevertheless
disconcerted to find she'd loomed so large and long and lush
in his imagination. What was it he was wanting?

Hard to say. War had made him more strategic. And what
might she make him? If they first met today, would even
their bodies speak? She thought so, maybe, way past flirtation,
drowned out by the cicadas, among the crass mimosas.

ROUGH

After the sightings, the sea got rough,
got rough on us, shale fallen to scarp and
shoving down, shunting against itself,
scathing and carping, flints striking flakes
off each other, sparking white, black, white.

Did I say sightings? I meant to say biting.
Nobody in beyond the ankle but
still that slash to the ankle bone, the sea
a sussurus of open-jawed serration,
strange voice at your ear.

Whatever we glimpsed out there hid itself
in potentia, flexing its muscle
under the water's skin. Head of a hawk,
head of a rottweiler. And the seals
in their slickers, black-backed, menaced

as we were, too doggish to know it. Her husband
lost like that, no longer the man she'd married,
but when were we ever? Nail head. Hammer head.
When will you admit you didn't know your own mother?
Strange mouth at your ear. Strange hand on your arm.

And did I say spiky? I meant to say spiny.
We could feel it under foot, every step
from the shoreline to the car. The sand
rough on us, the mind rougher.
Cross-cut saw. Shredder.

KING OF THE CATS

1

Who's Pavarotti now there's no Pavarotti?
Who's the new Yeats, now there's no more Yeats?
What was it Yeats said when Swinburne passed?
He said it to his sister. 'Now I'm the king of the cats'.

2

Once Caesar's stabbed, who bullies round the capital?
Twenty men on the ballot, all angling to be Lincoln.
Who crossed that river? Who swung that axe?
When the oak's brought down, every shrub looks tall.

And if we cloned Genghis Khan, would the new Khan
sweep through Asia? Would he cry – with Yeats –
    'Let all things
pass away'? The wind through the forum blows
    hot and cold.
'There come now no kings nor Caesars', wrote Pound,
    pre-Mussolini.

3

What was it the spirit communicators said
when Yeats thought his one first child might be enough?
They said, 'Your daughter's birth prepares the way'.
    They said,
'Your boy will alter time and times'. They said

'O Solomon! Let us try again!' They spoke thus
through the mouth of Mrs. Yeats. While scholars debate
the implications, in the audience Michael Yeats –
    that very boy –
holds his head in his hands – for all his birth and honors,
    not that child.

4

Is Caruso's son born singing, or born silenced? Imagine
    the strained
anticipation of his every burble and squeak. Can he,
    will he
follow along? Or consider the grandchild writing
    school essays
on her Gramps or Gran. Does she say what she knows
    for true – Gran

told me *this* – or hide what she doesn't? – arcane
    knowledge
or baffled incomprehension held equally close to the chest.
Natalie Cole, Sean Lennon, Jacob Dylan, Priscilla Presley.
The one thing they'll never do is sing just like their fathers.

5

'Funny thing', says the man, home late from the pub.
    The wife
looks dubious, strokes their drowsing tabby. 'Just now',
    says the man,
'a cat crossed my path, then another, and another –
twelve cats in all – till the last, this itty bitty kitten, says

Tell Tam Skattermiwaul! Tum Skattermiwaul has died'.
    You can guess, then,
who springs from the hearth, whose hair bristles out,
    who capers, who jigs,
who flies round the room and right up the chimney.
    You can guess
what's shouted, what's screeched. You can guess
    who's left open-mouthed.

6

The *Norton Anthology*, which footnotes even
Eve and Adam, footnotes Yeats too, in Auden's elegy.
    Paquin
once gowned the lithest socialites. Now she's a footnote
    to Pound's
Pisan cantos, and no one says her name or wears
    her brand. Who's Pavarotti,

my students asked last week. Who's Yeats? Who's Pound?
'Gone with the wind', writes Dowson, 'between the kisses
    and the wine'.
Who's Dowson? Who remembers? Something's tapping
    at the tables,
something's dragging at the pen, maybe it's Yeats himself

7

but who's to know? There's no Yeats left to listen,
no Pavarotti left to sing. Who's the new
Pavarotti? I can't think who.
My friends, there are no friends.

Note: 'King of the Cats': 'My friends, there are no friends' echoes
Jacques Derrida in *The Politics of Friendship*, where he echoes Montaigne
echoing Aristotle; or – for another source entirely – Coco Chanel.

DREW BLANCHARD

Drew Blanchard, born in Dubuque, Iowa, is the author of the chapbook, *Raincoat Variations* and the full-length collection of poetry, *Winter Dogs* from Salmon Poetry. His new book, *Unquiet Remains*, is slated for publication in 2019 with Salmon. He holds a BA in Journalism from the University of Iowa, an MFA in Creative Writing from The Ohio State University and a Ph.D in English from the University of Wisconsin-Milwaukee where he was twice awarded The Academy of American Poets Prize.

METANOIA

A sliver of bathroom light
divides my darkened room.
This ephemeral beam,
an obstruction that keeps
the dark from reaching dark,
is not a mystical vision, not
a simulacra or beacon,
but a simple focal point,
a place to rest my eyes,
a temporary stay of resignation
from sleep's uncertain shadows.
This is my month
of atonement. As I lie
on my back in the dark
and begin to contemplate,
chart the map, order and rate
my list of recent sins,
I'm interrupted by warm
September gusts that lift
and then release the rolled-down
window shades: each breath, exposing,
in syncopated glimpses,
sheets of low rain-clouds
above the silvered streets.
I rise and make my way
to the window. I hesitate,
then pull open the shades
onto grey light; restless,
the city dreams in fits,
tosses, turns, and kicks
to car-horn-alley-drop-off beeps.
In this moment,
considering again
my map of transgressions,
the difficult terrains,

the navigational tools
needed to begin
reparations, I'm shook
by my fears and the angels
as they make their way in
to me. Their eyes
glow inside my body.
Soft they say. *Soft* I say.
Inside historicity's
darkened rooms,
histrionically I burn
car tires.
Soft they say.
Soft I say.
My eyes close.
Their metronome-breathing
slows until I am a warm,
blanketed child.
Soft I say. *Stop* they say.
I consider the years
they're breathing
back into me.
I live in fear,
I fear my leaving.
They leave in long
black cars. They live
in shadows. I live under
street corner lights.
They live on police
station walls.
They swim in ocean
motel pools. They leave
slate-colored-lipstick-kisses
on cheeks, on mirrors.
I taste their absence,
their tongues and cigarettes,
each chipped and dirty

fingernail. The angels
no longer inside me,
I look onto wet everywhere.
Nobody's walking.
Nobody's falling.
Nobody's driving
drunk or singing.
Nobody's thinking
about killing
or mowing lawns.
All is wet.

STALKING

How strange to see my soul
floating in fields
of September corn. It was not
my dream to rustle
barely perceptibly
among the dead stalks,
to understand a moth's flutter
as the size of my forever.
My modified dream: To fold
my new existence
into origami variations
until I shudder into sound
enough to rise
starlings from stalks,
forcing murmurations –
a choreography-of-capture –
for the eyes of highway drivers;
the attention-snare
set to hold them –
rapt in the syncopated dance –
just long enough
so they cannot help
but recall the schools
of fish they loved
to watch on viral
YouTube clips, *Finding Nemo*
or childhood-aquariums-trips.

No Delicacy
for Jim Chapson and James Liddy

As I flew from the bicycle
         into a field of stone,
  I knew there was
no perfect way
        of remembering,
            no way
        of unbreaking things.
  I know you want
        the news, James,
            the tales,
        my escapades
with the French and Russian,
  the lady from Lima.
  Believe me, there's plenty
    of gossip to share,
but my notes
    are hidden well.
The photographs?
  Already sold.
  Your San Francisco
Beats and verbal beatings
    agreed that two wheels
    are no way to travel
on any road. As I flew
        through the wet-white air,
            I found a new
        frame of reference,
but managed still
    to contribute nothing new
to our understanding
    of centrifugal forces
nor the test of flesh
against the impenetrable
    magic of stone.

Travelling through the air,
           though, is never
really flying: We know that gravity
           turns airtime into mathematic
equations that equal falling.
           Try this: without
thought or hesitation,
           jump from a distance
that scares you. You will land
before you feel fear or pain.
Put your hand on a stone
           and you get to know
           the cold beauty of life.
           Put your hand
in the dank, dark earth
           and you get to know death.
Put your hand in water
and you see Gerty MacDowell
           on Sandy Mount and get wet.
Jim, James, I know this
           is not funny. Jack Spicer
radios us: Transistor,
           transmissions, transistor:
                Let go. The rooms
           need furnishing, James.
The furniture is disappearing.
           Suppose I didn't land
in a field of peat and stone,
           of blood and bone, and we landed
                in Morocco for a week of brown
           drinks and yellow food
           and unclean hotel rooms.
When we left County Clare
           there was the normalcy
of climbing stairs.
           Before I drove away,
           I waited for you to ascend,

for your light to click on.
That night, I knew the rooms
were furnished, the radio signals sent.
As I flew from the bicycle
I saw small swarms of gnats
in the evening sun, agitating
themselves and the world.
When I landed in the field
of peat and stone I knew
that I would never see
two shores as clearly again.

ROSLYN BLYN-LADREW

Roslyn Blyn-LaDrew began teaching Irish Gaelic at the University of Pennsylvania in 1990, and also teaches for the volunteer organization, Daltaí na Gaeilge. She has co-authored the Irish textbooks *Colloquial Irish: The Complete Course for Beginners* (Routledge, 2008, 2015) and the forthcoming *Colloquial Irish 2*. She writes and reads poetry in both Irish and English. Since 2009, she has been official Irish blogger for the language software company, Transparent Language. Other publications include *Clóicín Dearg*, an Irish translation of Little Red Riding Hood, and 'Geoffrey Keating, William Thoms, Raymond Williams, and the Terminology of Folklore: 'Béaloideas' as a Keyword', in *Folklore Forum*.

'SÉ FÁTH MO THURAIS

Is deas é an clog aláraim
Méileach na gcaorach
   Thíos cois na trá i nGaoth Dobhair. Dobhair
Is deas fós an suantraí
Glaoch na bhfaoileán
   I mBinn Éadair amach os mo chomhair.

Ach is deise i bhfad
Fuaim labhartha na ndaoine
   A chluinim istoíche isló
Gaeilge bhinn bhlasta
An bhfuil aon teanga chomh snasta?
   Bainim triail í a labhairt leo.

Glór na seandaoine
Ag insint na Fiannaíochta
   Achan fhocal ina sheanfhocal féin,
Lán de chríonnacht na haoise
'S an teanga sa chroí acu
   'S an seanchas a tháinig ó chéin.

An ghlúin sin i lár
Atá ag obair go dian
   Le fuadar is flústar gan sos,
Clann óg le díonadh
Boilg le líonadh –
   Ach coinníonn siad an teanga ina mbos.

Ach is binne agus is aoibhne
Glór na n-aos óg
   A bhfuil an teanga ar bharra a méara.
Má shéideann siad uirthi
An labhrófar fós í?
   Nó an ea nach labhrófar ach Béarla?

THE REASON FOR MY JOURNEY

'Tis pleasant to waken
To the bleating of sheep
   Down by the coast in Gaoth
And pleasantly soothing
The seagulls of Howth
   Beloved by poets of yore.

But how much more pleasant
The sound of the speech
   Once distant, now very near,
Sweet accented Gaelic
So polished and flowing
   I've traveled so far just to hear.

The voice of our elders
Whose stories of Fionn
   So eloquently his world portray
The wisdom of age
And the language in their hearts
   Would that their voices could stay!

And that generation
Who works like the dickens
   With pressure and stress far from calm,
Children to care for
Meals to prepare for –
   But the language they hold in their palm.

But sweetest of all is
The voice of the young
   Gaelic perched on their own fingertips,
If they blow her away
Will she see the next day
   Or will just English remain on their lips?

Is deas é go cinnte
Méileach na gcaorach
    Is glaoch na bhfaoileán sa spéir,
Ach is deise agus is binne
Gaeilge a chluinstin
    Ag na glúnta ar leo í go léir.

'Tis certainly pleasant
The bleating of sheep
   And the call of the seagulls in Howth
But it's finer and sweeter
To see Gaelic as leader
   In a land which practices both.

ÓID DO CHOMHAINMNEACHA DÁTHEANGACHA (*LE CÚPLA GAOL SAN ÁIREAMH*) / ODE TO BILINGUAL HOMONYMS (WITH A COUPLE OF COGNATES THROWN IN FOR GOOD MEASURE)

I'd sail the seven *seas* to **seas** by your side;
I'd *teach* you **teach** for house, if you'd open the door wide.
No need to *fear* that **fear**, he's really very nice;
Ríse's not for the guru, just for the color of the *rice*.
Dul's far from *dull*, it will take you where you want to go;
Do do isn't a misspelling for the poor extinct *dodo*.
Do shows what's yours and **do do**'s is for who you give it to,
Mo shows it's mine, and don't say '*Moe*' or we might think
     you're a stoo(ge).
And **bean**'s the word for woman, nothing to do with *beans*,
And **fan** is 'wait' or 'stay', *fan* isn't what it means.
'Don't be **mall** if you want to go with me to the *mall*,
I have to leave on time, so come on, let's go, y'all!'
True, we've got **mata** and **hata**, but we drop the 'a' for **cat**
And **bata**'s not like English – unless you use one for a *bat*.
But still there's hope, and that's no dope, **banana** means banana,
And **bandána** is almost the same as the English word *bandana*.
'I'll drive the **carr**, you take the **bus**', and let's find some
     more cognates,
So **gram** is *gram* and **Mam** is *Mam*, and **stáit**, well that
     means states.
I hope you liked this little **rann**, and no, that's not the
     word for *ran*,
A **rann**'s a little poem, so rhyme that one if you can.
If you read your **clann** a little **rann** – **as Gaeilge** – every day,
They'll soon be speaking Irish as quick as you can say
'Jack Robinson' in English – or to say 'as quick as a flash',
Try **ar luas lasrach** and your Irish will **teacht ar ais**.
So don't despair, don't say 'alas', when pondering **ciall na
     bhfocal**,
Just read these puns, and try to laugh, it's OK to chuckle.
Learning words is a life-long task,
If you don't know what it means, just ask!

Glossary/Gluais (*in order of appearance*)

seas	stand
teach	house
fear	man
ríse	of rice
dul	going, to go
Do do	for your
mo	my
bean	woman
fan	wait, stay
mall	late, slow
hata	hat
mata	mata
cat	cat
bata	stick (noun)
banana	banana
bandána	bandana
bus	bus
carr	car
gram	gram
Mam	Mam, Mom, Mum
stáit	states
rann	quatrain
clann	children, offspring
as Gaeilge	in Irish
ar luas lasrach	at a blazing speed
teacht ar ais	come back, coming back
ciall na bhfocal	the meaning of the words

HAIKU WRITTEN WHILE TEACHING A CLASS ON SEAMUS
HEANEY, 8 MARCH 2014, HARFORD PARK, RADNOR,
PENNSYLVANIA

Heaney hovers here at Harford,
Far from his farmhouse home,
The world mourns.

THE WHOSE-BREASTED WHAT-BEAK?

The rose-breasted grosbeak
Has no red on its head.
If the grosbeak's well bred,
Its breast's red
instead.

MATTHEW BOYLESTON

Matthew Boyleston is Associate Professor of English and Writing and former Dean of the School of Fine Arts at Houston Baptist University. He received a Ph.D in creative writing and literature from Houston and an MFA from South Carolina; he's taught at the Malahide Language School in Dublin; he works closely with Writers in the Schools. Boyleston's *Viewed from the Keel of a Canoe* was published by Educe Press in 2016. His poems and essays appear in *Confrontation, Spoon River Poetry Review, Blackwell's Companion to Creative Writing,* and *Puerto del Sol.* He lives in Houston with his wife and two daughters.

At Howth Head

I breathe in all the light I'm given –
the rhododendrons and the lesser auk,

Carrickmore and Kilrock,
the wide circle of a kestrel in the air.

Across the bay, the sea is as still as bone china.
The blank dark of Mt. Snowden winks at the sun.

I sit and watch the wither of a rose in an old garden
and remember a faint melody I had forgotten:

My one love said to me.
I sang this to my child every night of her long illness.

It is stuck like love in my throat's nib.

COTTON FIELD

My car clicked off, I climb barbed wire
and sludge into the muck of a freezing field
my family owned for years. Before he tired,

my grandfather drove a baby blue Ford
with a pistol beneath a pillow to scare the crows.
He ran his mouth like he drove. He peeled

pear after pear, hollered at his sows,
bragged of cancer, smiled big, and came
close to being a silly man. I was

embarrassed whenever I heard his name
but soon found out that there's a hitch:
all fields are born into the world the same –

as land shaved of baby pine and scratch
and end as broken cotton on frazzled branches.

A LITTLE BIT OF NIGHT MUSIC

Tonight there is no music:
a crescendo chaos of traffic sounds,
sirens, ground littered with pummeled stomps,
the repeat of a headboard on a wall.
And all that rumbles into screech and clack
is like a nocturne blistered out from Chopin's palms.
Someone grunts, the late night hiss of evening news,
a door slam, a dog's wail, and the wind
throws branches at the windowsill.
Tonight my mind is like a reel-to-reel.
You flicker back and forth in a stranger's bed.
Our sharp words skip like a scratched CD.
And I see your leavings around my house:
old clothes, hair ties, a tampon's slip in tissue in the trash.
In a helmet of smoke, by myself, I cannot still.
I shake through every moment's space.
And the single things I cannot understand
are cymbals, scissors on a violin,
the tensions of an out of tune
guitar and at every car I rush to hear
you shut your door, and every car moves on.

~

With the music turned so low,
I can barely hear the outline of a phrase,
thin as bowstring or an old strand
of your hair my pen has gathered in its nib.
I listen to a volumeless storm unfold,
the Elgar Concerto for cello,
beneath the arms of Jaclyn du Pre.
At this pitch, she's delicate as candle flame,
no intensity of movement or *sturm und drang,*
or even the tremolo, like yearning, of a string.
I would have it this way always –

with just the lisp of music, or the hiss above the lisp –
a faint, tempered tempest barely daring
to tremble or to sway. Nothing of her highs or lows,
swapping man for man, mania, MS, not a thing, not death.
Nothing of the fullness of a sound-house
alive in the abscess of her legs,
knowing when full things are made thin,
without passion, we're assured
this thinness will keep us living
like a thinness in our blood.

~

In the world according to Bach all anger is polyphonic
and the cello splinters into violins.
In the Double Concerto, we are the *largo ma non tanto* –
two wooden bodies set to chin,
Stern and Pearlman fighting in canonic form,
in discourse with the fragments of a turning phrase,
repetitions of familiar themes
(you're drunk again, who is this man?).
Has all our conflict come to this –
two voices forming music neither can possess?
The concert ends in the *leibestod* of a hoarse Isolde.
Curtain drawn, the rumble moves to the vestibule
where chatter clinks louder than a champagne glass.
The orchestra unravels itself.
We're like the pins-and-needles of our legs,
asleep, on edge, pricked full of holes. The quiet grows.
You're cold and bored and leave to mingle with the distant
roar, but now settled I strain for any sound
left pacing in the air, the laughter of the cast backstage,
strain to hear the lost echo of one overtone,
the silver drone of a French Horn blown in tune.

~

We feel all things between us merge
into a score, like the words of Mahler
that the symphony is a world
where all discordant notes have found a place.
When we are stretched out
on my couch like Scheherazade,
our toes touch Tierra del Fuego,
our hair falls dark on a tundra,
and our one waist traces an equatorial line.
We contain all that is possible
of voice and sound and this *Eine Kleine
Nacht Musik* found locked in an armoire
in Salzburg or Vienna,
those scattered fragments of a fifth movement
that linger like a phantom itch
in Mozart's score are played before us,
and our random darkness becomes whispers
from another room, voices through a thin wall.
We are grounded into music.
We whisper Mahler.
We fall asleep in the throats of each other.

REHABILITATION

The water rustles like taffeta.

Veteran, newly crippled,
he clings to the dock's edge
one-armed and squinting eyes.
He mutters to coax his stiffing limb:
a splintered board lashed to his side.
He is pinned into a man.

Once the dock was on floaters.
It bobbed as we ran to dive.
In storms it was a tongue of the earth
lapping the water like a dog.

Aluminum poles the man at the store
swore would not rust support it.
The delicate tissue of styrofoam
has vanished and the wood
rots on its eternal crutch.

He grips the sides, treads to a towel –
thirty minutes a day, every day, he swims.

I see the dock needs a coat of varnish,
and it chips in the wind.

RAND BRANDES

Rand Brandes is the Martin Luther Stevens Professor of English at Lenoir-Rhyne University in Hickory, NC. He received his BA from Hanover College, and his MA and Ph.D from Emory University. For almost thirty years Brandes worked regularly in Dublin with Irish poet and Nobel Laureate Seamus Heaney. He has published widely in contemporary British and Irish poetry. Brandes is the Lenoir-Rhyne Writer-in-Residence, and poems from his chapbook *Balefires* have been translated into Romanian by Nicolae Dabija. His chapbook *What Winter* was published in 2010 by Goosepen Press in 2010 and *seen unseen* with photographs by Fanjoy/Labrenz in 2011.

COURTING THUNDER

Midsummer is the flowering season of the oak,
which is the tree of endurance and triumph,
and like the ash is said to 'court the lightning flash'.
– Robert Graves, *The White Goddess*

When the lightning unzipped our tree
The bark fell off like a new bride's dress
Sometime after clock-stopping mid-night
The flash and thunder blew us out of bed
Twenty-five years after we planted the oak
Thirty feet from the window we knew
Was too close, but we wanted to watch it
Grow until it blocked our view and cast
Its great shadow over the world below
In the summer and etched the earth in winter.
So we wait to see if it was a death-blow,
If the leaves will fade before the fall
If the birds will fill in for them perched
On branches and limbs. And yet
There is the outside chance that the bolt
Did not reach the heart of the tree
And that the sap just exploded in line
With logic and luck. Perhaps when spring
Comes new leaves will come too and all
That we will feel is the long scar forgetting
The shock of that night, thanking the stars
For a second chance, for thick skin, and love.

WINTERING OUT IN SARAJEVO

So cold that war
Winter, they burnt
Their books, not
Wall by wall,
Or case by case,
Not even shelf by
Shelf or book by
Book.

No, with shaking
Hands they read
Each page as if
Committing a crime
To memory,
Then ripped it
From the spine
Joylessly.

THE WEANING

It was the first lie I ever told you
And you do not even remember it
Or know it. All you will recall

Is the space that opened between
Us and a grief so deep
And nameless that you broke

Into tears over heavy sighs,
Sobs, as if you wanted to drown
Yourself and the world in pain.

This was your baptism, as real
As when you broke into my life
Crying between my thighs, then arms,

Then breasts not knowing
That you could never return
To the warm, sweet river that flowed

Through, not me and you, but us
Comingling and consummate.
 Pulling away, I lifted your sweet face

Making sure that you would survive,
Were breathing, and that I was breathing
Too, sharing the same broken breath

The same truth and knowing
That I had done the right thing.

THE CARD I NEVER SENT GEORGIA O'KEEFFE

You've seen it all before, how the river gorge
Folds in on itself, reds and roses and pinks

Sinking into soft pools still as the forgiving fonts
In an ancient V deeper than time before men

When all there was and will be is woman
Opening herself up wide to the world

Your brush wet with the colors of wonder
Surrendering nothing, yielding everything

In Love's Canyon …

THE LAST CLASS

I want to leave them, them to leave me
Feeling the poems' pulsing lines in their veins
Hammering at the forges of their hearts,
But it's just 'Intro. to Poetry' and they've already sold
Kinnell and Collins, Hughes and Heaney
For 50 cents each to the college bookstore.

The room has grown silent and sleepy in the late morning
Light. Papers are piled precariously on my desk,
Titles peeping out like 'The Illuminated Blake',
'Lawrence's Ladies' or 'What's Eating Plath'.
Not wanting it to end like this I impulsively pull out
'Great Poems Read by the Great Poets Themselves'.

Slipping the disc into the slot and hitting play
Yeats chants, Thomas rages, Williams chatters,
And then Kinnell, the last poet, the last poem,
'The Last Gods' – a poem I do not know,
But should have. Suddenly the goddess is spreading
Her legs as the sea surges around the rock

Upon which she lingers, the god wades out to her
Sliding blueberries and blood between her wet lips.
Mortals that we are, we sit silent, embarrassed
By the gift we have been given in communion
In a classroom on a Tuesday in December.
This is what it's all about, I say, the power

Of words to call forth a love so elemental, so powerful
And profoundly deep, that we must, like Stephen Dedalus
On the strand, exclaim 'O' Profane Joy' as the bird girl
Wades forth lifting her dress over her ivory thighs.
We have been blessed, I say again, blessed.
They say, that's great but will it be on the test?

The Rain Stick Revisited
for Seamus Heaney

I gave you a rain stick
And you gave it back
In words all sluice rush
And downpour and glitter-
Drizzle – a virtual exchange.

What does an Irishman
Need with a rain stick
When you have twenty-five
Words for rain – pissing,
Lashing, spitting, and soft.

Absurd as it was and without
Irony you accepted the gift
That keeps on giving until
The player or the played
Gives in in diminuendo and dust.

So upend the rain stick again
My old friend wet from birth
And listen for what water
Has to say about the next time
Around and giving and forgiving.

CACTUS

Three thousand miles and north of Sligo
I meet, again, the strangeness of *cactus*.
The word sticks in my throat
As I remember your cactus too,
So out of place and odd
Standing desert green in the window
Of an old Indiana farm house.
'Cactus', I say, licking the blood
From my little finger.

HEATHER CORBALLY BRYANT

Heather Corbally Bryant teaches in the Writing Program at Wellesley. She received her BA from Harvard and her Ph.D from Michigan. Her study *How Will the Heart Endure: Elizabeth Bowen and the Landscape of War* won the ACIS prize. She's published seven poetry collections: *Cheap Grace, Lottery Ticket, Compass Rose, My Wedding Dress, Thunderstorm* (nominated for a Massachusetts Book Award), *Eve's Lament* and *James Joyce's Water Closet* (awarded honorable mention from Finishing Line). *Island Dream Songs* will be published in 2019. Two of her poems – 'James Joyce's Water Closet' and 'The Easterly' – were nominated for the Pushcart Prize in 2018.

FLAG IRIS ON OMEY ISLAND

We reach Omey island late on a June afternoon when
    the sun has been up for days – we have all been
Expecting rain and so this sunshine comes as a surprise
    – we cross the packed sand, exposed at low tide,
Knowing we have

Only so long to explore before waters will begin filling up
    the shore – we pass Connemara ponies grazing
On high grasses, painted white gates to nowhere shut tight
    – only a few other walkers have braved this
Trespass to this island

Caught in controversy – where coffins are still carried
    across the sands to be buried in the remaining
Churchyard where others fought to reclaim the land,
    dotted among the landscape clumps of wild yellow
Iris, flag they're called

In Ireland – part of the landscape – they grow in wetlands,
    bogs, marshes, and ditches – spots of sunshine,
part of the family of Iridaceae, joyful, jaunty.

Matters of death, and of eternity are more matter
    of fact here – life is
Hard and lived close to the bone, a meeting
    of tragedy and comedy, a
Story in every glass – we don't find it easy to accept
    this honesty, this
Clarity – there is no mincing of the truth, except for the
    great unspoken.

In Tullycross church we learn the coffin maker
    lives down the street –
His children grew up jumping in and out of coffins
    in the making – death
Is close to life – the priest asks us to pray for those
    in need – I think of
Catastrophe and bravery, forbearance in the face of
    great pain, prayer.

In the Letterfrack Schoolyard

A sunny morning, in early summer – I sit at a picnic table
    slanted with
Shade, listening to children playing in the schoolyard –
    their laughter
Falls out of windows, adjacent to the tall stone school, circa
    1887, where

Atrocities occurred, scarring the land, built on an island
    already filled with
Scars and sorrow, a land always caught up in someone
    else's war – no
Repair can be made for the history, one that led at least
    one hundred

Boys to their death – only seventy-four bodies recovered
    for burial,
Form B filled out in duplicate, or triplicate, death
    from poverty, flu,
Tuberculosis, or the unmentionable: extraordinary cruelty,
    pervasive neglect.

TENTH SUNDAY IN ORDINARY TIME, ACHILL SOUND

On Achill Sound I enter a church for a service, the first
    in perhaps a
Decade – I slip among the parishioners, unsure of what
    to whisper
Or how to pray – sometimes I see religion like insurance,
    perhaps it

May help, come what may – and yet, at the same time,
    my pleas seem
False – why should God listen to me in this place
    by the sea? We are
Cordial to God's vision, as the priest exhorts, perhaps
    he will be

Granted a mission to heaven – sometimes I don't know
    what to pray
For – there are too many things – and I end up deciding
    not to take
Communion, though the wafer could slip through
    my fingers with ease.

I light a candle after the service has ended, whispering
    one quiet hope.

The storm lashes out as soon as the ferry docks – we
    slip on seaweed
Steps as we make our way to the only café we see –
    a blurred dot in
The distance, accessible by foot – inside, we are warmed
    by cappuccino

And lattes – yet, outside the storm gathers – we don't even
    know it has
A name, but there we are, thrust into the elements –
    the wind is so
Strong we can dance – if we stretch out our arms we
    can be pinwheels

Lifted by the wind – caught in a flurry of gusts and bursts
    – Grace
O'Malley's castle shields us from the gales, windows
    barred from entry.

MIDSUMMER PICNIC, CORK

The college warden passes by our picnic on
    the green lawn,
Telling us to put away the fifths of gin we are slugging,
Washing down our cheese, crackers, grapes
    and strawberries –

It's been awhile since I've saw on a college lawn
    and chatted
With a group of women, some I've known
    for awhile, others
I have just met – it's been an eventful afternoon – another

Friend has taken a terrible fall – we've seen brambles,
    barbed
Wire, and green ivy climbing on secret garden walls,
    the softness
Of the afternoon blurring some of the harsh history
    that once

Preceded it – the sun climbs high in the sky, the light
    staying
As long as is possible on this lush and luscious
    summer night.

SIOBHÁN CAMPBELL

Siobhán Campbell's awards include the Oxford Brookes International Poetry Prize and the Templar Prize. Recent collections include *Heat Signature* and *Cross-Talk*, with lyrics termed 'torpedoes lined with feather strokes' by Bernard O'Donoghue. Her poetry is widely anthologised: *New British and Irish Poets* (Bloodaxe) and *Womens' Work: Twentieth Century Poets Writing in English*. Campbell co-edited *Eavan Boland: Inside History* (Arlen House, 2017). Her critical work appears in *The Portable Poetry Workshop* and *Making Integral: The Work of Richard Murphy*. She teaches in the UK at The Open University where her research into creative writing practice takes her from Northern Ireland to Lebanon and Iraq.

The wishes of sheep are inscrutable except
when they run uphill at any alarm as if they
recall a great flood, or dash through a gap
as one entity afraid to be caught.
When they prop against a gate post, sheep
discover their nethers tingle when scratched.
They like to watch bees suck pollen from
thistles, seeding us more clearing work for spring.
Their different-toned bleating, infused
with a yearn we can't always hear, is how
they re-tell almost everything. They can smell
when water goes putrid so they favour the copper-
bronze stream, feeling its minerals feeding
their brains. *A running brook, though you visit
again, is not the same.* One flock will believe that
that lot next door have butterfly minds –
have nothing to do with them. They have a hauteur
they cultivate with their lambs even while letting
them play. As adults they sometimes pretend to
fight; it passes the day. To us, they all seem the same,
even though we remember how shearing sheep
for the first time, seeing their yellow lozenge eyes,
the way they looked into us, threw us asunder.

NIGHT LIGHT

Here's to the workers, the benders, the binders
in their slow push across the open field
moving and planning as if all is certain.
We wanted none of that,
tucked under the sweeping ash
on grass that would never be hay.

We thought we knew best, lolled till the night
closed on the day. And then we saw it –
lantern of goblin, flicker of demon,
spittle of devil, will-o-the-wisp.

Did you come to let us know the worst –
spin us a fright at the light that teeters and dips?
When we move, you move.
No way out but the gate in the side of the field
where you lie in wait.

Are you a person lit from within with a hope
or a beckon? No limbs but a head that
flickers and bobs. What do you know of the ways
we have taken?

We can be punished, streaky with sweat
on our backs on the grass that can never be cut.
We can learn how things must always fit together.
Will o the wisp o, wisp o the will o
we will repent in any given future
if you'll just let us go, o will o the wisp.

HERDING

is not what we call it on the scrubby
dairy farms west of the Shannon
where you need twice the acres
for every cow and calf.
And they must be intrepid, check the edge
of bog pools for safe footing,
watch how bulrushes hold tufts
of sweet scutch between rocks.

But out there with the collie, counting
the browns – compact with muscle,
the black and whites – elongate and awkward,
can feel like riding out a range –
complete with hoof-beats
keeping time with time.
I know their breath is warm even
when a spring day falls cold.
And the dog, useless as he is,
under the illusion he is working.

Rain on Us All

on those who vote, and on those who don't rain
on the polls, the streaming posters, the puttering balloons
rain that will keep them away, the old and infirm
those who can't stray out for fear
rain drops unnumbered, why do we think you are for us?

rain on the mines and the mine shafts, the slag heaps
and the one they flattened that killed the children
rain on it not being there
we cannot be neutral in rain, we are for it or against it
rain demands an opinion
is it wet enough for you?
rain on you then

rain is not a belief, it does not take sides or whip up a spin
it is not a sin to believe in the rain
or even to think it is good
and not just for ducks or frogs or rivers or streams
play is called off for rain
race meetings cancelled, the money stalling, the
guesthouse closed

rain is not a persuasion
but it might begin in the end to persuade
if it wasn't there and the livestock were slaughtered
for want of water
rain needs respect and respect will it get
from you and you and you who make laws
and are getting wet
from you who are wet

rain of the records, how many we kill on our roads
or who we send home after a fall
it's cheaper for us if they die in their homes
rain on the boy who got into the school

and on those who did not
rain on all of the waiting lists
starting to rot

rain tries to talk to the spokesman at briefings
so we know what we know but
the rain is knowing, it touches us there and there and there
reaches to places we've half forgotten

rain no less and no more
what's to be made of it?

or so it seems as she takes her place behind him,
two cow lengths away but alert to changes of direction.
Her eyes are brown he thinks, *if I were asked* –
all her kind have the same bog pool eyes.
He knows they are oval, not round, with a crescent
of white if she's not feeling right. She won't look at him
straight but sways her heavy head to see all things.
They do this walk down and back for milking. He moves
the gap in the hedge from time to time but she always
knows, waits for him on the other side. At night
he thinks he sees her pupils shining when he opens
the back door. From a field away he reaches
her disdain. Tomorrow they walk this way again.

CHRISTINE CASSON

Christine Casson is the author of *After the First World*, a book of poems. Her work has appeared in numerous journals and anthologies. She has also published critical essays on the work of Leslie Marmon Silko, Linda Hogan, and Robert Penn Warren. Ms. Casson is currently writing a book of non-fiction that explores the relationship between trauma and memory, and is at work on a study of the poetic sequence entitled *Sequence and Time Signature: A Study in Poetic Orchestration.* Her second book of poems is forthcoming from Salmon Poetry. She is Scholar-/Writer-in-Residence at Emerson College.

THICKET

In his garage daylight skims brackish shadow,
those tools he always used silenced, labor
stalled by limbs turned in increments to stone,

chores postponed. The hedge trimmer nestles
on a low shelf, cord dressing the bald skull
encasing the motorized brain. Cradling

his arm, she helps him along, steps precise,
deliberate, his balance compromised.
'I'll show you how it works', he advises,

knowing it will be useful in his absence,
lifting it from its niche, his stiffened frame
still strong, and she, suppressing her alarm

lets him have his way, follows him outdoors.
His awkward gait's a warning she'll ignore
against her judgement, knowing the import

of this one last grasp at independence,
the burgeoning shrubbery a nuisance
he could remedy with rapt attention

to his work – so different from years before
when she as a child, determined to walk
the playground's steep wall, had no fear of harm,

her hands out-held in counterbalance,
proceeding carefully, each step buoyant,
and he below, easy in his presence.

Now, she eyes him closely as he levels
the droning cutter at twigs emboldened
by neglect; tilting it till it nips, whines

and spits them out. The power line twitches
in the grass. 'Let me try' she says, watches
as he releases the trigger. Blades coast

to a halt. She places her hands where his had been,
takes up where he's left off as he looks on,
and swears she will manage the job this once

as he would – dismissing the vibrations
riddling her wrists, the stems' recalcitrance
stuttering and fueling its puckish gnarl

till she is done. Then 'let's go inside for lunch',
she says, leads him to the house, the silence
relaxing his rigid posture, the tenseness

of his gait. She knows he might fall backwards –
follows tight behind him up the porch stairs.
The table's been set. She's prepared and dressed

a salad he can eat, busies herself
with sandwiches, and from the pantry shelf
takes down the strange powder that will quell

his dysphagia, keep liquids from slipping
down his larynx to his lungs, three scoops stirred
into every glass. The carton reads, *Thick-it*,

into 'nectar', 'honey', 'pudding', by degrees,
his apple juice transfigured as she pours –
to denser texture, slow, coalescing –

certain, like those neuro-fibrillary
tangles suppressing his will. She will
keep him safe. She'll watch him without looking

while he eats. Later, she'll clear the table,
fix to dry in the rack, his glass, the plate,
as he waits in his chair, patient, settled.

The Lift

Falling backward, puzzling us all, but doctors
grasped what ailed you at last, your symptoms troubling,
adding up, revealing your certain crisis –
    ravelling brain cells,

muscle palsy, walking a sudden challenge,
eyes unfocused, swallowing risky; balance,
speech disrupted. What could we do to keep you
    sheltered, your body

over-burdened, stiffening limbs arrested?
Transfer chair, slip-free floors, a walker, grab bars,
extra railings, wheelchair – aseptic, sterile
    gadgets to help you

bathe and move on your own. We waited, careful
not to let you know as you worsened, daily.
How to keep you home when you couldn't manage
    stairs to the bedroom?

There, in the ad – a chair lift – *powered motor,
sturdy seating braced on a heavy railing* –
what we longed for, steel bough gesturing upward,
    raising you, faithful,

skyward, yearning for transport, captive. Drive-wheels
whirred you up flights and down endlessly, placid
escort. Mechanized Sisyphus. Newfangled
    fellowship – steadfast –

narrow seat embracing you, plastic, womb-like.
Hoisted, lowered, what was it like, this planet's
forces averted? Your imminent landing?
    Energies mastered,

easily once you clambered ladders, roof-bound,
clearing gutters, replacing shingles, keeping
house for years, and gravity patient, waiting,
    tugging you downward

slowly. Now you aspirate liquids, breathing
matter, wrenching it into air, each inhale
lengthened. Craving freedom, you crawl in darkness:
    adamant, alone,

vexed if we hamper your progress, tolerance
waning. Days you are pliant, obedient,
suffering shrouded. Today you persisted:
    death is my answer.

Tired, weighted, breath of dust lures you closer.
Illness obliges to ferry you earthward.
Wordless, you leave, shattering space. The chair-lift –
open-armed, vacant.

Needle's Eye

Those small petals you lavished on me, tossed
casually, landing in my hair, from the plants
I bought to flower even in shade brimming
in spite of pinched light, they'd fallen out last night
when I brushed them free. They lie there still
where I left them, neither curled nor dried
but miniatures of themselves, accomplishing
in their immanence what my mother insisted
on her last day was necessary for the world
to become what it should – everything made small
as though diminishment could make departure
easy, or easier than it otherwise would be.

'Everything needs to be tiny, make it tiny',
she said, calling from her bed, her breathlessness
set aside for once, her voice carrying across
the room, down the hall, calling you to the doorway
and I lying beside her, trying to see
what she saw, her eyes focused beyond the wall
where what was small could find a place to rest.
For years her life had narrowed, pulled close
by her refusals of the world – her inward drawing –
as ordinary tasks became more difficult:
groceries, laundry, keeping house, washing
herself at day's end, the appetite she'd force.

It's good to think of silence, the after-music,
but to what end? What lies aside these sounds
that fall so close and fast? What's warranted?
assured? Philosophers, mystics would take us
to an other home where melodies spin –
ciphers indecipherable – where worms
turn and turn again, digest, regurgitate,
informed by the maw that keeps us treading
on a mill. Is this beyond? A place

furtive as the mouse behind the wall,
the plasterboard and nails starry-stalled?
revelations custom-fit to compensate?

These broken corollas: raiments, remnants,
perfected. Pink medallions reduced,
intensified, settled on our floor.
We should sweep them away. Holding on,
my mother told me that a graying woman
wheeled her past her mother's dresser, her own,
then my father's, circumambulating
the bedroom. How she asked you in a dream
to shut tightly all the closets, windows, doors –
alone, isolate, but for her mind's guide:
the threshold of the room, the needle's eye
where all contracts, inbreathes, constellates.

BRENDAN CORCORAN

Brendan Corcoran completed his MA in poetry writing at The Johns Hopkins University Writing Seminars before moving on to Emory University and a Ph.D in Irish and British twentieth-century and contemporary poetry. He has published poems in *Cimarron Review*, *Nimrod*, the *Bellingham Review* and other small outlets. Currently an Associate Professor of English at Indiana State University, he works on twentieth-century and contemporary Irish poetry, the elegy and the intersection of literature and climate change. He has published on the poetry of John Keats, Seamus Heaney, Derek Mahon, Michael Longley and Ciaran Carson.

You would have loved this house, its stubbornness,
Sheer volume, the individuality
Of every door's dimensions. Wavy panes
Of glass so slowly flowing towards long-settled
Foundations. Solid brick walls that yet breathe.
The damaged plaster vaulted ceiling whose
Broken scalloped beams extend their horse hair
Into a roughly finished lacuna.
Long corridors echoing with your grandson's
Bare feet racing towards imaginary rooms.
I surprise myself sometimes thinking of you
And what you'd say about the latest concern
With the roof, the shifting stairs, only to snag
On the fact you were gone before we moved in.

FOUND POEM: JUTLAND CIRCA 290 BCE

Emmer, spelt, bread wheat, rye,
naked barley, hulled barley, cultivated oat,
wild oat, green bristle grass, cockspur, timothy,
Yorkshire fog, tufted hair grass, common reed,
heath grass, wood bluegrass, lop grass, common rye grass,
flaxfield rye grass, couch grass, oval sedge,
field wood-rush, curled dock, sheep's sorrel, pale
persicaria, redshank, common knotgrass,
fat hen, goosefoot, common mouse-ear chickweed,
common chickweed, lesser stitchwort, annual knawel,
corn spurrey, meadow buttercup, creeping buttercup,
common fumitory, field pennycress,
shepherd's purse, wallflower, cow parsley, field
mustard, parsley piert, silver cinquefoil, tormentil,
field clover, lesser hop trefoil, flax,
field pansy, field forget-me-not, self-heal,
common hemp nettle, black nightshade, thyme-leaved
speedwell, rattle, greater plantain, ribwort plantain,
clustered bellflower, yarrow, scentless mayweed,
nipplewort, autumn hawkbit, spiny sow-thistle,
narrow-leaved hawkbit, smooth hawkbit, and pig
bone fragments. Grauballe Man's last meal.

(Pauline Asingh's *Grauballe Man: Portrait of a Bog Body*, 90)

NOVEMBER SUNSET

Ocean pH has fallen by about 0.1 pH unit from preindustrial times to today ... [This] is equivalent to about a 26% increase in the ocean hydrogen ion concentration. If we continue on the expected trajectory for fossil-fuel use and rising atmospheric CO_2, pH is likely to drop by 0.3-0.4 units by the end of the 21st century and increase ocean hydrogen ion concentration (or acidity) by 100-150% above what it was in preindustrial times.
– *Scott Doney, Senior Scientist, Woods Hole Oceanographic Institution, USA*

Late November and the crows
Are settling in for their over-wintering
In and around town. Evenings,
When a still yellow sun looking warm
Drops into those aqueous sunfish hues
Inflating the west, starlight delayed
A moment, a flare's arcing whistle
And crack (quieter than it will be at night)
Punctuates random traffic
And the joyfully arbitrary flight paths
Of hundreds of crows overhead,
Unperturbed as they cavort and gyre,
Careen and cry out to it all well above
The empty canopies of their gypsy roosts.
How viable this sky at evening looks,
Here or elsewhere – over the sea,
Waves done in charcoal and ink beneath
The blaze of loveliness indifferent utterly
To the grave below the rapturous surface,
Inside the horizon itself. Sterilized
Acid silence. Stillness save for the bulbs
Of titanic jellyfish pulsing translucently.

OUR FIRST DIVE

Sitting together high up the concrete slope
Of the not quite empty stands,
Heavy misshapen chunks of snow falling
Vertically, their almost audible concussions
In the slush distracting us from the last game
Of the season, you seem smaller now
Than how I saw you earlier: a big-for-your-age
Five-year-old stretching upwards within and against
the door frame to which I am duly fitted and hinged,
your father. Today you just seemed smaller
as we huddled beneath an umbrella covered
with sea turtles, our feet cold, your thigh against mine,
A brick of heat, while I hoped I too might be able
To keep you warm as I explained the rules
Of the game. We left for the car just before halftime.
The engine idling, heat up high, you pressed
bare feet against the registers in the front seat.
As we warmed up before driving down the street
For a hot chocolate and heading home,
I watched your feet soften like butter
Making it to room temperature and
I was sadly glad for our car, its cabin almost hot,
Despite your incredulity the other morning
After we had heard Jacques Cousteau's granddaughter
Admit that she no longer likes to dive
Because so little of what she's known
Underwater remains. Alexandra Cousteau
started diving at seven. You pricked up your ears at this
Because I have promised that when you can swim
Laps and are legal to dive (age thirteen),
Together we'll get certified and find a reef
Still full of life and breathe underwater
Agog at the mystery and abundance
Before it's gone. The morning after the lecture
You asked what has happened to the coral.

On the way to school, I told you
And about fossil fuels and carbon,
Planetary warming and acidifying seas.
You just asked: why then do we drive our car?

SNOWFALL

1

Which is heavier? A pound of lead or a pound of snow?
My son's science joke reminds me that in the magic
Realm of a vacuum, a lead weight and a snowflake
Fall at the same rate. And I remember my own
First contact with such physics, finding it hard
Not to imagine some playful force hauling
The snowfall down while an opposing gravity
Pressed back against the lead's dead weight.
And so, it snows today: lazy crystal parafoils
Dropping from the flittering air, the whitening
Ground blending with the sky, all that is lead
And leaden pushed back, momentarily.

2

Sledding last winter after a barely adequate snow,
Mobs of kids and parents tramping the hill,
You balked at a headfirst dive to the bottom,
The ice grinding harshly like gravel or sand
When your ear's so close to the ground. Instead,
We rode down together, side-by-side, one of us
Spinning deliriously in the saucer. Or sharing
One short foam board, you tucked in
In front, me pedaling with my hands then holding
Tightly onto you. This winter, the headlong rush
As you raced your friend came readily; from up top,
I saw you even catch air off the teenagers' ramp.

WONDERLAND

A week into his summer holidays,
my son woke up today with
'the best dream ever'.
He'd had a twenty-four-hour day at the playground
with his two best friends.
But, being 'the best dream ever',
the playground was really a space ship.
And once the boys entered it
without any qualms, they found
neither aliens nor lotus flowers.
Here, was every playground you could ever imagine.
And so they played.
And every LEGO you could ever imagine.
And so they built.
And every game you could ever imagine.
And so they gamed.
And every TV channel you could ever imagine.
And so they watched.
And every pasta you ever imagine.
And so they ate, of course.
When time was up and the day was over,
dads arrived in our very own spaceships
and took the boys home.
Mine was neither distraught nor exhausted,
just confirmed in his ninth year
and ready to start his day.

TYLER FARRELL

Tyler Farrell received his undergraduate degree at Creighton University, where he studied with Eamonn Wall, and his doctorate from the University of Wisconsin at Milwaukee, where he studied with James Liddy. He has published three books with Salmon – *Tethered to the Earth*, *The Land of Give and Take* and *Stichomythia* – and contributed a biographical essay for James Liddy's *Selected Poems* (Arlen House, 2011). Farrell is currently a Visiting Assistant Professor at Marquette University where he teaches poetry, drama, film, writing and literature and leads two study abroad programs, one to Ireland, the other to London. His Morrissey imitations are said to be legendary.

James Joyce played entrepreneur
on Mary Street gaslit Dublin 1909.
He wrote narrative and poetry, made
silvery memory images young actors
kissing rain drops, dancing with canes
outside shop windows. Zeal conquers
all and magic contains no tricks. For
the world needs movies now more than
ever to entertain all Catholics bored
by sermons, all filled with Christ's love
warm gleam floating beneath blue skies
trees in full leaf. We demand moving
pictures, fierce words to roam in our
hearts, comedies and tragedies playing
like children in the streets of Dublin.
All 20th century poverty will be over-
shadowed by soft legend and the sleep
of gods. All lights will imagine music
in the depths of our souls. Who cares
if no one really understands the medium
of film? You will educate all of Europe
agendas dissolving like grey darkening
glow of the electric theater. The surface
of the sky will simply ply us with rhythms
flickering sleep disappearing like a sunset.

On Seeing the Druid Theatre's *Waiting for Godot* in Galway, 2016

Wait and stop the long line
of silence – makes me cry
the seats mingled with dirt
rock, those boots alone
empty in the universe. Tears
over joyed with final touches
among the living, darkness
enlightening life is and love
is and time is for all of us.
Days we look for help take
each other over large bodies
of water makes us thirsty
the day and the night, moon
glow muse shine. I waited
in line some minutes for a ticket
rush and glass in hand, stage
manager hat with red flower
hair led me inside chambers
dusty world news. Motionless
and feverish I stared with
mouth agape at players
poets in word trance. Stillness
sounds from pain killer beat
like leaf tree and those beams
of desolation human light
forms. Isn't it obvious! Some
dramas unfold slowly and
grown out worth the weight.

Do Not Speak of Rain

speak of fire.
Our lips are warm
currents running
to and from
beaches spread
out near vast oceans.
Make trenches
with your hands.
Bring water
to fill them with
passages like ripest
fruit. Our intimate
experience forges
public creation. For
privacy falls
between rain drops.

Nature is evidence
of us, symbols
like birds in flight.
Do not bury them
in holes, plant them
on tops of towers flying
upwards toward
heaven.
Grasses rise at night
ancient Spain
expresses strategic
body art.
No, do not
speak of rain. Water
can only darken
the clouds.
Near us always blows
the fearful away.

POWER OUTAGE IN MILWAUKEE

Sudden shock
lights extinguish.
Here run the days
of rain
and thunder.
Spark gas stove
and candles. Kitchen
smells of apples
glows like lanterns
in the grey.
We cook, stir
hold each other
with answers.
Climb basement
stairs, unwind
the flashlight.
Careful steps, hand
holding, quick
flash kisses.
Your daughter
wanders close
steers us with feet.
We check the fusebox
switch flips
epiphany. We could
be like this our
entire lives.
Sudden large light
ignites our insides
knowing looks.
Minds illuminate
with strike flare flash.
Electric love in the darkness
our body thoughts
capture the lightness.

Croque Madame for you (egg over easy, slightly runny)
crab cake BLT for me (grilled and bacon smoky). Sharing
bites a must! Smart set converses, orders together craves
lovely glances green eyes among teal walls soft opaque
noon-light. Glances, holding hands under tables fates and
muses sing songs, feed us words like food from wonderful
gods. What we add to the menu? Daily specials brightly
thru windows and dark dressed waiters who know us by
name and poem, our choices. We drink, spread tangy
mustard senses tingle like hearts belief in mysterious
regions of tasteful bodies. What to order next time – crab
wedge oyster Caesar with grilled romaine, lobster roll –
exotic food tantalizes us like rare birds while paintings
hold lovely flowers. Taste impact the flow of centuries
lunching together lingering. Gather us like power of
meadows, searchlight threading sound. Together we touch
smart goodness with our lips prepare to breathe in our
luscious language orchard.

3 Basquiat Postcards Written to Andy Warhol

1

Red ginger, ostrich plume ginger colored eruptions
Mauna Loa Volcano Maui unlike dark grey spray can
streets covered red paint fire. SAMO 1940, 1955, 1984
famous for football helmets. You are here I am not
send money for the same old shit hello to the freezing ones.
What value drawing send 10 dollars for the paint
13 cent stamps across the pacific to Pittsburg
4 sets of 20 home on time we are separated into 4s
TV party interviewed late night picture frame
when artists dance the mad wind.

2

Self Portrait makeshift canvas fridge
door translucent foam metal sheet rock.
Fingers always covered in spray paint
video installation. Black still dripping
from graffiti art in galleries video poetry
multiple choice questions late night
public access golden wood junkie.
Interview self-sound art school followers
safe as houses plush drunk people donate
Polaroids - plates and markers. Black
stars and crowns drowned in vase water.
Teach us the history of money shine
and race paint Armani suits with bare
feet. We all need famous friends like
Keith Haring and urban wonder. First
youth production like Avant Garde rock
band identity is 10 dollars for a birth
certificate from Puerto Rico and Haiti.
Mental illness, addiction collide in the
underground sewers of New York, New

York. Dutch pink new wave music digging
colors. A A B B rope hip hop beat bop
album art door on head 393 and collage
pieces shine at every corner a mirage.

3

Mirrors and vodka aural blue ear freezing. Invitation
for the world human race and gender boxing gloves hold
    up the sky.
Ghana's on the phone with skinny per capita false teeth.
Friends crowed the heir apparent – 4 styles of jazz. Bebop
    mother
Matilde taught him look like a shaved goldfish. Ancient
    myth
African rock art Venus of Willendorf and Titian
where we motor area Times Square. Alchemy and Liberty
    circa 1500.
Bullet and skull bone, Egypt's dark river where barren
    trees
shadow ivory sugar. Notebooks are filled with psalm
and prayers in mono, a place to dry out in time for gallery
openings. One word, for poets shape history and all souls
before him and artists before and after this time. Stay
    shelter
recruiting drums beyond the horizon of setting suns,
    golden crowns.

DEBORAH FLEMING

Deborah Fleming has authored two poetry collections, *Morning, Winter Solstice* and *Into a New Country*; two chapbooks, *Migrations* and *Source of the River*; a novel, *Without Leave*, winner of the Asheville Award from Black Mountain Press; and a non-fiction collection *Resurrection of the Wild: Meditations on Ohio's Natural Landscape*. She has published scholarship on Yeats, Jeffers and Synge. Winner of a Vandewater Poetry Award and grants from the NEH and NCLS, she has had three poems nominated for the Pushcart Prize. Currently she lives on a farm in northeast Ohio with her husband Clarke W. Owens, also a writer.

WOLFHOUND

His long back stretches out
as legs measure off the furlongs.
Created for Roman warfare,
bred to hunt wolves in Irish forests,
he now chases rabbits
made of steel and pulled along a wire.

When he stands on strong hind legs,
his shoulders reach much higher
than a mastiff's. His coat is smoky
gray like the Cliffs of Moher.

Head upon his paws, lying beside the fire,
he is a vision loosened from his epoch.
The room unfolds around him
in a tapestry.

THOROUGHBRED

Raised for the oldest sport of man,
most finely bred of all his kind,
he is a legend written into land.
His graceful neck descends to his long back
above the cave of lungs, coursing
river of his heart; long tapering legs
and rounded haunches pull the ground
behind him, every stride a wingless flight.
You think: speed, bone, blood. Even words
we use to talk of him take us back
a century or two, suggest a life of leisure –
furlong, downs, jockey, stakes, rail;
his names raise flesh and tingle
in the scalp – Nijinski, Man O War, Citation,
Sea Bird, Hyperion, Nasrullah, Secretariat;
his places strut their pageantry–
Circus Maximus, Hippodrome, Hialeah,
Curragh of Kildare.

Canvases of history are painted
with his image: any rider seems
a conqueror on his back,
the servant a master,
so exquisite the legend
he creates of man.

SKELLIG ISLANDS
County Kerry, Ireland

At the end of land the sheer rock spires
rise dripping from the water. In legend,
they were steps a giant sowed upon the sea,
a pathway to the under-wave;
they became a fortress for the learned
seeking visions in a desert
until marauders overran it;
then they housed a beacon
bringing ships to land.

Now, waves blossom into kittiwakes,
cormorants, and gulls, original inheritors
claiming back their birthright,
knowing that the sea will give them
all that they can ever need.

SEA OTTERS

Where are the coats greedy men
Sewed from their luxurious skins?
Hunted to near extinction,
They fed on spiny urchins
That consume the coral garden
Where iridescent sapphire fish
Weave among branches out and in.
Now, whenever they wish,

They float upon the calm sea-mirror,
And, as we beg them back again,
They plunge, and in an instant, disappear.

SONG OF THE GOAT

Tragedy: (Greek) *tragos* (goat) + *aeidan* (to sing)

You have called upon me in your time of need,
eaten my flesh, stolen my milk to feed your young
though my young starved, taken my skin to cover
your nakedness, stretched it over poles to shelter
your bare head, made my horn your emblem of plenty.
I was your shepherd and you called me Betrayer.

You placed upon me your grievous sins
and turned me into the desert to starve. I cleared
your pastures of weeds your cattle and horses
would not eat. You spilled my blood that your
firstborn might live, that your god might rise again
to ensure great harvest. You covered me with nerve

gas that destroyed my spine, watched while I died
in the fiery wind of your explosions.
When you see yourself in my eyes you call me clever,
remark my nature in yours: I am curious and sure-footed;
I learn quickly, resist fences, imitate my kind;
although I love the herd, I will leave it for better grazing.

I have asked nothing of you, but you take all from me.
My wild cousins scramble over mountain slopes
and gaze down on clouds unfurling. I look past you
to a time when you have destroyed yourselves with greed
and you call upon me for help, and I on the high peaks
will not answer and will never descend unto you again.

PHOTOGRAPHS

Wisps of cloud framed in the window
of an old brick factory, a relic.
Cumulus boiling upward from a wooded
hill, light reflected off the river
between branches of an old tree.
Even the pathway unfolds
like one of your poems,
leading to a new country where you
stride along the mountain ridge
above fields divided by stone fences,
northward the sea. On winter evenings
I still wear your old sweater,
read that poem of yours I found
in a journal, one you published
before we met and forgot,
discovered on a day of bright clouds,
like a memory rising unbidden
from shadows.

HERON

The sun has not yet climbed above
the hill that floats upon the pond's
gray mirror as the great blue
steps among the vines and briars
in the aspen-shaded shallows,
hieroglyph of the god of morning
with eyes that pierce the current,
shepherd's crook of his neck,
stilts like long reeds
that break the glittering surface.

Some movement in the thicket
and he sends out one cry
of *graak* across the water,
lifts into air,
spreading his wing-capes,
gray ghost dragging his feet
behind him to sail above the land,
ascending into ever-widening day.

DAVID GARDINER

David Gardiner is a poet and editor who currently lives in Chicago. From 2006 to 2010, he was founder and editor of *An Sionnach*, publishing Van Morrison, Seamus Heaney, Eavan Boland, Paula Meehan and Eamonn Wall. He has served as Professor and Director of Irish Studies at Creighton University, Burns Scholar at Boston College and UK Arts Fellow at the University of Ulster, Coleraine. For ten years, he directed the Creighton summer program at Trinity College Dublin. He has authored over 60 journal publications and five books, including the poetry collections *Downstate* and *The Chivalry of Crime*. His collection *Interstates* will be published in 2020.

ENTOMOLOGY: NATURAL HISTORY MUSEUM, DUBLIN

Italian, Polish & silly laughter at tit birds
fill the dead zoo. I head straight by
kits perpetually at play back to the hawk moths.

Pink & green & ridiculous, they're mounted under glass.
I think of them hovering around foxgloves,
scolding me for drinking their nectar out of fuchsia.

Looking for that iridescent green moth again,
I realize I know nothing about them. *Noctuidae,*
hemiptera and even *callophrys rubi* seem all the same to me …

Then I hear a couple call a mountain ringlet 'boring'.
I want to turn on them & tell them, 'the last one,
the last one, was taken at Lough Gill in 1895,

that whatever their gropey, bored hands think,
this single blue-brown moth hasn't been seen in a century'.
But they're gone too. I'm left with the *true bugs*.

Smashed capsids & a hilariously mounted leafhopper
now have me pinned here in the back of the museum.
There's nothing boring again.

By the time the kids have bought their plastic animals,
I'm leaning on the case, laughing at myself in love
with the cock-chafer's eye-lashes, rose-chafer's shell –

the delicate beauty of the tortoise beetle;
all the delineations & small wildness of a world
we hold forever in our hands.

THESE DARK PLACES

I have shown you all my dark places –
rooms where blinds are permanently drawn,
end tables & armoires you simply sense are there.
The smell of lavender & cedar provides small welcome.

Your hands felt what your heart didn't know,
navigating sharp edges & silent spots.
Your hands felt what my heart didn't know –
that the room may fill with light, fill with flowers.

You have seen all of my dark places.
Your having left, I twist the blinds open,
sense the dust unsettled, hear your footsteps
down a hallway that I can't find in the dark

stepping over the broken vase, looking out,
I want to show you the flowers on the wooden floor.

Her teal crocs squeak on the gallery floor.
Her new glasses match the bell jar
of Degas' *Dancer* replica cast in Omaha.

'What position is she in?' I ask her
after we back away from Pissarro
as much to make sure that she has the right glasses

as that she might remember something
that I know after I have to leave her again.
She counts, tongue in her teeth:

'one, two, three ...'

Stone City, Iowa is a gallery
away from us & I've told her &
her sister about 1930,

farm failures around here,
Iowa, why his trees look like
brussel sprouts, the stubborn idealism

that all will be well. I'm lost though.
'Fifth position!' Phoebe says now.
her hands are back, chin proud.

I hug her, hold her big sister's hand &
walk through galleries of cinnabar,
heroes & villains of the 17th century –

all galloping off of their gilded frames,
towards some green ideal distance
where princesses dance without instruction

and good princes stand waiting in sunset.

FROG'S LOVE TO THE SCORPION

We swam the creek together.
I took your love, assurance &
you to my heart.

I said I thought I had wings;
didn't know what they were for.
You laughed with me.

I took you onto my back
where you slept. I felt the weight
of your troubles.

I thought we'd nearly made it.
Then I woke you to your self.
Then it went wrong.

I made two mistakes with you.
My second one was my first.

After you stung me, we drowned.
I loved you the whole way down.
I love you still.

I remember what you said:

This all does not concern you.
None of it is your issue.
It is just in my nature.
I will love you forever.

I hear this as salt waters
hold me again quietly;
close around me.

PRUNING
for Olivia

I had to leave in May, roses blooming
& both of my daughters crying, running
through the yard after the car.

There was nowhere for me to go,
then or now; the blank, empty sun
& long Omaha nights that summer.
In the rearview, I watched life foreshorten.

I feel stillness in every quiet afternoon
their tears & arms outstretched still.
It's a distance that I might never map;
a late warm distance I can only feel.

That whole first summer Olivia kept
the roses that we planted together
along the front walk – teas and hybrids.
At ten, she stubbornly knew how to trim them all.

She searched without gloves through thorns for
the three-leaved joints & the early deadening pods.
Throughout the long summer nights and storms,
she would sneak out in her pajamas
with my clippers that she hid.

She didn't tell me until she too had grown.
Mostly, I remember the weekend she learned
to ride a bike & fell into those roses.

I wish I could have comforted her those nights
checking for thorns & protecting her
the way that I did that day & always hope to.
She taught herself not to be scratched as she stared

for indications in the dark; places to be trimmed,
made to grow through her love, memory & attention.

Her hands are mine. She tended to my heart
as she made the roses grow & held
my temperamental shears in her hand,
returning them to the empty half of the garage.

THE STAY

I am at your bedside & you are the only one
who doesn't know that you're dying.

You are asleep but wave to me at one point.
I want to talk to you about everything now,
right now, before the doctor comes in &
tells you that you're dying.

We'll never have a normal conversation again after that;
I'm wondering now if we ever did & wondering
    why I hold this.

I want to stay this moment of execution.
I want you to wake. I want you to talk to me &
I want it to be like it was two hours ago.

I want so many things but mostly for you to live.
For now, I settle for holding your hand & asking

the doctor not to come & God just grant that.

RENNY GOLDEN

Renny Golden's latest book of poetry, *Blood Desert: Witnesses 1820–1880* (University of New Mexico Press), won the WILLA Literary Award for poetry 2010–2011, was named a Southwest Notable Book of the Year 2012 and was a Finalist for the New Mexico/Arizona Book Award. Golden was nominated for a Pushcart in 2016. *The Music of Her Rivers* will be published by the University of New Mexico Press in fall 2019. Golden is a professor emerita at Northeastern Illinois University.

SHAKE DOWN THEIR SONGS

I

I know County Kerry in dreams as if Pa and Ma's childhood
belonged to me. Their laughter in a flat on Dante Street, a
chime the wind rings. Their brogues, a cadence of rain, brooks.

We walk from mass past bungalows and weed lots.
Pa in a wrinkled suit: 'Monseigneur's a stuffed shirt, Missus'.
Ma: 'A gentleman, Dinny, not your Mick *boyos'*.

In the parlor a tenor sings *Oh the Days of the Kerry Piper,*
the dance of farmers whose language was forbidden.
They dance as if their bodies can outrun darkness.

Stomp, whirl past grievance and what they've abandoned.
They dance to remember, then to forget. They dance
for their lost valleys. They dance their way to heaven.

Now I hear a brogue in a crowd and turn as if I could call
them out of graves, shake down their songs like apples
from the orchards of time. All they left, never left.

II

I, too, knew how to leave. Don't look back, I told myself,
squeaking through marble halls in black-heeled oxfords.
In a year, snow whitened the Motherhouse, dusted
    Michigan barns,

the amputated cornfields brittle and dazzled. I made vows
when summer lifted its antiphon of cicadas and warblers.
A white veil, the Great Silence, bells that refused excuse.

A cohort of nineteen-year-olds from Irish and Polish ghettoes
whose laughter saved us from the scorch of discipline.
Not so much in rebellion – but irrepressible joy.

There were leavings, old nuns we loved. Sister Anna.
At dawn our river of veils and white floor-length habits
followed the coffin. Her sack of holy bones listened

as we wove into a cemetery with its circle of stone markers
singing *In paradisum deducant te Angeli*, May the angels
lead you into paradise – you, Sister, who asked so little.

III

When I left, Dylan sang 'A Hard Rain's Gonna Fall'.
America on the bridge, floodwaters rising.
So much washing away, what could I hold onto?

Not the church with its admirals sailing the ship,
women below in steerage. I had no ambition
to go above deck. Instead I left.

In El Salvador during the war, I was baptized again.
I knelt in a Mejicanos church smoked in candle-light
and prayed for Brigido, a catechist, to hold out.

Hung by his wrists, forced to squat for hours,
cut, cursed, bloodied. He gave no names.
Everything immediate as a bullet, a *comunidad*

that had power but could not save anyone.
Stubborn hope like a shudder of stars hung
above killing fields. No way out. Only each other.

V

Now the graveyards of Chalatenango.
Their unremarkable crucified sleep
beneath white crosses and plastic flowers

where farmers fled B47s that blew them
into clouds. Their song, though, was indestructible.
Forty years later it rises above the *campo* and slum gullies:

Cuando los pobres crean en los pobres
ya tendremos la libertad. When the poor believe
in the poor, then we'll have our freedom.

I kneel, hear their voices fall through dust showers over
a silent field, its fuego trees, sonsonate birds that skim
cornfields where the poor, who believe in the poor, blaze.

REPUBLIC STEEL MEMORIAL DAY PICNIC, 1937
for Denis Murphy of Local #399

I

What he remembered of his union days
was that day in May in an industrial park.
The camaraderie. The odds. The bloodshed.

Slow afternoon, dumb with spring air. Sam Otis's boy
tugs a kite in a cobalt sky. It floats above tilted
beer barrels, horseshoe pitchers, above the Calumet

river which winks from shadows as if it, too, had
a holiday. The boys' shoes are dusted gold from dandelions.
Sunlight ordains blast furnaces, the dark arms of cranes.

When police circle that Memorial Day picnic, men form
lines, a sun-mottled army of white undershirts, red and black
suspenders. They move as one in front of their families.

Tension runs the line the way a bass pulls tight,
the hook tearing deeper and deeper.
Strikers wait for the circle of blue shirts to loosen.

When Captain Mooney orders the police loop to tighten
everyone bolts, a thunder of feet kicking past wicker baskets,
plates of beans, sauerkraut, pig knuckles and fried chicken.

Shots split Leon Franchesco's faded work shirt,
a stain opening like a rose. Sam Popovitch can't run fast.
He falls holding a smashed skull, his dying eyes astonished.

An accordion winces where they push Dolan from
      a line of shots.
Workers pull the fallen Sam Causey into someone's car
but cops drag him bleeding back onto the street.

Otis Jones and nine others will not see the strike end.
Otis's boy runs ahead does not see his father's crumpled body.
He looks up to see the kites fall slowly, crookedly.

II

Seventy years later, we stand in a union hall by a faded
    Republic Steel sign.
Wood stage creaks, a ratty velvet curtain for backdrop.
Ed Sadlowski says 'We'll never forget what happened here'.

Old men clap, shift weight, lift trembling fists, sing
    Solidarity Forever.
They shuffle to the catered luncheon, eat pizza
at dark tables, then walk into the afternoon where once a
pale sky rained kites helpless in the plundered air.

City of Big Shoulders: An Anthology of Chicago Poetry, 'Republic Steel'
University of Iowa, ed. Ryan Van Cleave

WHATEVER YOU SAY, SAY NOTHING
– Seamus Heaney
for Maggie O'Connell Golden

Maggie arrived in Chicago's bully hour
with nothing to match its glare.

Her floppy wool hat announced old country.
Union Station was a merry-go-round of Yanks

in dark suits whirling past the sixteen-year-old.
America, she saw, rode a fast horse.

Maggie stood stiff among strangers shooting past,
gripped her suitcase as an anchor.

Alert for her sister Katy's brogue – calling
Maggie, Maggie as if something had ended.

                    *

Maggie had left Cahersiveen and the weedy coast
where her distant relative, the great Dan O'Connell's

Derrynane stood imperious, a smoke-stone great house
that faced the bay's sand-paths at Ireland's edge.

Derrynane was below Macgillicuddy's Reef where, across
three heathered fields of matted sheep, stood Maggie's cottage

that held her O'Connells who slept with goats in two rooms.
Her father, Michael, in the salted air of farmland

heaved sod from rock soil as if time were a landlord.
If her quiet father complained, Maggie and her sisters

remembered little, so erased were their own worries.
What voice would Maggie bring if not the voice

of women who owned nothing, not land,
or history which belonged to orators and rebels.

Maggie's American home was void of Celtic symbols
as if she forgot or carried her first lesson –

silence and invisibility. No Irish knots
announcing her country, herself.

There was Irish women's art: Maggie's crocheted lace
doilies lay on armrests intricate as small flags of surrender.

Maggie gave six children the soul-gift of kindness
and the talisman of quiet and courtesy.

Whatever you do, make no fuss.

Julie Henigan

Julie Henigan, a native of southwest Missouri, holds a Master's in Folklore from UNC and a Ph.D in English from the University of Notre Dame. She has published journal articles on subjects ranging from the *sean-nós* tradition to Joyce's 'The Dead' and Synge's *Playboy of the Western World*. Her poems have appeared in a number of little magazines, including *Outposts, Orbis,* and *Irish Studies South*. A singer and multi-instrumentalist, she performs traditional Irish and American music, with a well-received CD ('American Stranger') and two guitar books to her credit.

DYING FOR A PEE

It is Ireland,
where people seem to have
the continence of camels,
for no bus boasts
conveniences
and public lavatories
are a thing of dreams.
I am on the non-stop
bus to Limerick,
doing the penance
of the weak-bladdered
for the sin of using
public transportation.
Now Limerick
has become for me a shrine,
where the station toilets wait
in blessèd cubicles,
and holy water
will bestow on me at last
its tender mercies
for this pilgrimage of pain.

CHORA SFAKION

As we sat one evening on a rock in Crete,
gazing across the Milky Way
towards Africa,
the moment hung about us
like a flock of gulls,
hovering – never quite at rest.
In that immensity of sea and sky,
fear and consolation seemed inseparable,
the two sides of a coin continually tossed
by some uncertain god,
first destroying, then restoring,
as the waves lapped at our feet.

THE CHINESE MOTHER'S LULLABY

Come along, my wee piglet,
till I kiss your hoofeen.
I wind one wee toe and another wee toe;
bend this little piggy,
bend that little piggy;
there's a naughty wee piggy a-sticking out so!

There, there, *a thaisce*,
there's work to be done.
Itty toe, bitty toe, wee digitalis;
Fetter for a little calf,
Hobble for a hen,
Swaddling of silk
for your feet, my dear one.

Though a little jaybird she,
my girleen will walk abroad
like bamboo on a windy day,
like a willow wand.
Bend big toe, bend little toe:
all wrapped up neatly –
a lotus new-closed.

There's flat-footed Clíona
And splay-footed Máire;
Peigí has flat feet
and Niamh's feet sprawl.
Keep still, my darling,
with my hand on the swathing;
it's Mammy who loves you
and keeps you from harm.

– translated from the Irish of Biddy Jenkinson's 'Suantraí na Máthar Síní'

SWEENEY IN GLEN BOLCAIN
(after Seamus Heaney's 'Sweeney Astray')

Making my escape
from one place to the next,
harried by the wind and snow,
by enemies and friends,
by hungers
that can never be fulfilled,
I come to rest
by moonlight
in the one place
that I love.

Having nothing left
is not a hardship here.
Not reminded of
the things I've lost,
I think of what I have:
this view, at midnight,
of glistening streams
and branches
heavy with solitude.
I make my poems here,
singing them
to birds, while time,
for just this little time,
stands still.

My time in green Glen Bolcain
is never long enough.
Naked and frightened from my wits
I shall fly too soon
from its cool shelter into
things unknown,
into chaos blacker than the
blackest night.

Spurred by fear,
by sharp necessity,
I shall never grow complacent here;
never know peace,
but for a space –
nor grace
until I die.

This was the curse:
that I should henceforth
know no rest,
but utter lunacies to birds,
make verses for the wind and sky –
no more to know the comfort
of the stay-at-homes,
of those into whose windows
I can only gaze
with fear.

I am alone and mad.
Yet when I'm in Glen Bolcain
the pain abates, the torment eases,
and my frenzy passes
like a summer storm. I see
as no sane man has seen
the red of rowan berries
and the white of hawthorn buds;
the glint of salmon
leaping in the streams
that quench my thirst
and cool my stinging brow;
blues and every kind of green
in the flickering leaves
that shade the brooks
and give me shelter
day and night;
the blinking light of stars

upcast from ice-black
streams at midnight:
these have I seen and felt.
The very stones have
offered up their secrets,
and the tress have given
me their songs.
In turn, I give them words
and wait for rescue
which I know will never come:
for I am Sweeney,
alone and mad,
cast off for saying
what should never have been said.

One day, perhaps,
I shall repent the words
that brought upon me
Ronan's curse;
but never will I cease to rail
against the fate that brought
me to this end,
to fashion verses
borne upon the wind
to parts unknown
and ears deaf to my torment.
The cold moon rising in Columbcille
and going down in Mourne,
the muttering of owls,
the keening of hounds,
and the chant
of waterfalls in the icy glen –
these must I write
in runes
upon the wind:
a madman's litany
for saints to profit by.

With the sky for my psalter
and branches for my hermitage,
I will say the wild prayers
of my office, and only Moling,
at the last, will hear.
My soul will perch
above him at the well,
then fly
where even that holy monk
can't catch me,
scattering words
as thick as leaves
and dropping them
like stars
in the dark pools of the glen.

PATRICK HICKS

Patrick Hicks has authored over ten books, including *The Collector of Names, Adoptable, This London* and the acclaimed novel, *The Commandant of Lubizec*. His poetry has appeared on NPR, *The PBSNewsHour* and *American Life in Poetry*. He's received awards from *Glimmer Train,* the Bush Artist Foundation, the South Dakota Arts Council, the Loft Literary Center and the NEH. He was recently a finalist for an Emmy and he hosts and curates *Poetry from Studio 47*. A dual citizen of Ireland and America, Hicks is Writer-in-Residence at Augustana and teaches in the MFA Program at Sierra Nevada College.

THE STRANGERS
on the night my internationally adopted son arrived

After we picked you up at the Omaha airport,
we clamped you into a new car seat
and listened to you yowl
beneath the streetlights of Nebraska.

Our hotel suite was plump with toys,
ready, we hoped, to soothe you into America.
But for a solid hour you watched the door,
shrieking, *Umma*, the Korean word for mother.

Once or twice you glanced back at us
and, in this netherworld where a door home
had slammed shut forever, your terrified eyes
paced between the past and the future.

Umma, you screamed. *Umma!*
But your foster mother back in Seoul never appeared.

Your new mother and I lay on the bed,
cooing your birth name,
until, at last, you collapsed into our arms.

In time, even terror must yield to sleep.

When He is an Old Man

Long after my body has been turned into ash,
and his own children have walked into middle-age,
they will eventually gather around his hospital bed.
My son, an old man with papery skin,
will be hooked up to an octopus of machines.
Tubes will push fluid into his body –
his ribcage will rise and fall. His heart will blip.

He might be scared, but also content
with the arc and burn of his life.
I will stand at the foot of his bed
just as I did when he was a baby,
watching him breathe.

As nurses rush in for his final moments,
I'd like to put my cool hand on his cheek,
and whisper into his ear that his daddy still loves him.
If there is another life, I'll be waiting for him
just as I did at the Omaha airport when we first met.
I'll be the one craning my neck at the new arrivals,
waving my hands like crazy, ecstatic at last
to welcome him home.

TWIN CITIES
after Louis MacNeice

I was born in America, between New England and Hollywood,
between the slave trade market and the clang of streetcars,
then to the Twin Cities where snow falls deep upon
Norwegian immigrants, burying roads and cornstalk stubble.

Fields remember being stolen from the Ojibwe, they bristle
        with ice,
wolves prowl for meat as railroads judder beneath the moon –
clattering cars carry cattle towards streets named after pioneers.
The Mississippi starts here, dividing the land in two.

I am a silverfish that swims laps between my birth country
and my ancestral home, even as the ghosts at Fort Sumter
and the Boyne launch cannonballs overhead, I live beneath
        the border,
I skirt the nets of birthright and dart through silt. Like you

I belong in two places at once, but I am born of two colonies,
America and Ireland – twice twinning me to an English
        crown.
My upbringing in the Twin Cities of Minneapolis/St Paul
is a metaphor not lost upon my gemini flesh. You understand

what it means to live on these borderlands, far from the
        bog and cross,
the linen mills, baseball diamonds, and the fireworks of
        July.
I tread cultural binaries, my restless feet pace the cold
        Atlantic,
just as you tight-roped the Irish Sea, neither here

nor there. Our boyhoods were different, but we are both
        pulled back
to Carrickfergus in County Antrim, to a castle with

crossed-arms.
Between the twin cities of its Scotch and Irish quarters,
my ancestors sharpened their teeth, attached their bayonets.

You and I stand with locked shoulders looking out to sea,
thinking of Romulus and Remus, of how tight intimacies
breed division, we feel the loss of a home, which is no
    longer home,
as air from North America begins to lift our sail, once again.

TRYING TO PRESERVE BRIAN MOORE'S HOUSE
– *Clifton Street, Belfast, 1998*

What remained of your childhood home
was to be smothered under the tar of a parking lot.
There wasn't much left beneath the blanket of litter,
save the chequered mosaic of your kitchen floor.

You left Northern Ireland for North America
and now I, addicted to your fiction,
reach down through the years.
I bend low, and the crumbling fist-sized pieces
of your kitchen floor come to me easily.
Useful paperweights, I think. Literary history.
But the helicopters, steady as hummingbirds,
hang over this broken lot, watching.

I hear a waking bullet click –
and, still stooped, look to each corner
of your childhood garden. Nervous soldiers
raise their guns, the squawk of a radio,
my breathless chest in their crosshairs.

Time photographs itself.

Slowly, in glacial time, I pocket
your house and with surrendered hands
step away from the present.
I push through the defiant graffiti of
je maintiendrai tiocfaidh ár lá
and bring your past home,
to America.

A paperweight now, it guards your books
and remembers how you once scooted
over its polished surface – testing your rootless legs –
waiting for that moment, when you would walk away.

READING THE TÁIN

You would do for looking after men of poetry,
but you are a little young for dealing with men of war.
– from *Táin Bó Cuailnge*

So said Conall to Cúchulainn,
that bull watcher, hound splitter, chariot crusher.
Late in my education, he has come to me.
Achilles and Beowulf are dust,
Troy and Jutland, replaced by Ulster.
How odd, because Irish monks, those early scribes,
helped save that Greek and the Scandinavian.

Hunched over vellum, aiming the arrow tip of a quill,
these men lettered the lifeblood of literature.
With crushed pigment and beeswax,
they dreamed myth onto stretched calfskin,
they sacrificed flesh for the love of words.
Had they known that other legends
would one day overwhelm Cúchulainn,
would they, these men of poetry,
invite the bull watcher to safeguard
their herds of precious calfskin?

Would they warn him that foreign men –
warriors with strange names and gods –
were riding to the Battlefield of Vellum,
that ink would flow like blood?
Knowing this, young Cúchulainn
might scan the foggy horizon,
sword in his fist, he stands now,
waiting for the world to be written.

THE ROAD CREW

It's July, the temp is pushing 107º,
and men in reflective vests move around
greasy yellow machinery –
clumpy asphalt is poured out thickly,
scalding the air, making a kiln of the world.
They smoke cigarettes, and laugh
at the ground trembling beneath their boots.

Near the sidewalk,
three boys on dirt bikes demolish ice cream cones,
they watch the work of men and listen to hard words.
When they're done, fingers licked clean,
they push off and ride a lip of cooling asphalt.
Once or twice they glance back at
the snake marks their tires make in the road,
a road they have only just begun to travel.

Credits:
Cold Mountain Review: 'When He is an Old Man'
Finding the Gossamer: 'Twin Cities' (Salmon Poetry)
Poetry City, USA: 'The Strangers'
Studies: An Irish Quarterly Review: 'Reading the Táin' and 'Trying to
Preserve Brian Moore's House'

BEN HOWARD

Ben Howard, Emeritus Professor of English at Alfred University, is the author of eleven books, most recently *Immovable Awareness: The Intimate Practice of Zen* and *Firewood and Ashes: New and Selected Poems*. Over the past four decades he has contributed poetry, essays and criticism to leading journals in England, Ireland and North America. His honors include the Milton Dorfman Prize in Poetry, an NEA Fellowship and numerous residencies at Yaddo. Before his retirement he taught literature, writing, classical guitar and Buddhist meditation at Alfred University. He now leads the Falling Leaf Sangha, a Zen practice group in Alfred, New York.

LATE OCTOBER
in memory of John Montague, 1929–2016

Master of the lyric reminiscence,
you undertook to make of broken Ulster
a single, radiant, redemptive whole
and out of tales and songs long since dispersed
the noble arc of one coherent story.
Of Irish history you made a plaster
to treat your culture's long-neglected wound
and heal your own, as though the two were one.

In the old photo, you and I are walking
back from a swim in a frigid country pond.
Towels in our hands, we look restored,
as though the cold had cleansed us of our sorrows.
Your hair is white, mine a youthful brown.
Fifteen years my senior, you'd convinced me
against my cautious reckonings, to join you.
How crisp and bright, that day in late October.

ORIGINAL SELF

Where are you hiding, I have sometimes asked,
you who bear the name *original*
but have no form or formal properties
for anyone to grasp or call their own.
Filling my pen, my mind unduly vexed,
I think your habitat might be this inkwell,
its black, glassy circularities
suggestive of a vase or burial urn.
Blacker than black, the ink contained therein.
Let me not be troubled by the notes
my aging cells are sending to my brain.
And let me cast my lot with what I've written,
whether it vanish or with luck remain.
For this I draw on you, for is it not
your office to reanimate this pen
and leave behind a mark or lasting stain?

THE PLEASURES OF INSCRIPTION

Perhaps it was in my genes
or at least my heritage,
this urge to reify

the moment in a word
or fix in a radiant phrase
those shadows on the snow

shifting in morning light.
Or was it the urgent need
discovered early on

to rectify in lines
of verse the dark and fluid
disorder of the world?

How I would like to claim
a high, ennobling purpose
akin to Akhmatova's

or Pasternak's refusals
or William Dunbar's wish
to capture once and for all

the sadly ephemeral
nature of his art.
But truth to tell, this morning

I think it was nothing more
or less than these peculiar
pleasures of inscription,

which Hardy must have felt
and Sophocles before him,
even as they looked

on death and human passion
and faithfully inscribed
such words as came to mind.

THE SWUNG MALLET

Always the driving question: *who will win?*
Even in my dreams it animates
characters and scenes, impelling me
into a house or car or situation

I'd otherwise avoid. A god within,
it dictates what I think and what I state
to be the case, as though the mystery
of being could be solved by inquisition

and even the blackest darkness be dispelled
by acts of will. And yet this other voice,
so foreign to my native education,
calls on me to question why it matters

whether the swung mallet ring the bell
and why I should be subject to the force
of willful thought in league with cold persuasion
when such is not my wish nor truest nature.

GALLIARDS AND PAVANES

What was it drew me to those early forms,
to Dowland's melodies and Cutting's dances,
Rosseter's high-arching, plaintive phrases
no longer lightened by the dainty lute
but deepened by the voice of the guitar?
For years I played them, not quite comprehending
the gaiety that rises from despair,
the courtliness that soothes a broken heart.
Mastering the *Melancholy Galliard,*
I too was dwelling in the zones of danger,
the moment's beauty darkened by its risk,
the brevity of life more certain than its joys.
Little wonder they were often paired,
the one infused with reckless energy,
the other by necessity constrained.
Five decades on, I'm playing them again,
finding in their unexpected rhythms,
their heretofore-unheard-of harmonies,
a rich felicity suffused with sorrow,
a bitter ruth alloyed with bold adventure,
and, once more, the spirit of my youth
consorting with mature, unhurried motion.

CATHERINE KASPER

Catherine Kasper received her BA (and her pilot's license) at Illinois-Urbana, her MA from Illinois-Chicago and her Ph.D. from the University of Denver. Her books include fiction – *Notes from the Committee, Hovering, Optical Projections* – and poetry – *Field Stone, A Gradual Disappearance of Insects*. She wrote critical work on Steven Millhauser and on Barbara Guest and also served as co-editor of *American Letters & Commentary*, a journal which she helped transform into a book press. Kasper died in April 2017 from a rare form of sarcoma. She is survived by her husband, David Ray Vance. Poems here are from her manuscript *Future Beauty*.

'Daydreamers Investigate Morality' is constructed from the *New York Times* article of that title, November 1, 2003.

'Genome Sequence' is constructed from descriptions of Hussein Chalayan's conceptual and innovative fashions in *Hussein Chalayan*, edited by Robert Violette, NY: Rizzoli, 2011.

Cybernoun

It takes off before you can shut your mouth, finds its
    rhythm

in the drive of its own momentum, overwhelming
    associations

cylindrical, electrical, chemical

wired and piston-driven – amorous repetitive motion

slips along the groove of preordained rhythm

energy impeded by the drag of reluctance

The first word is friction, initial spark of *genus*

Festered in vegetative soil, glorious golem

winningly grinning, until it becomes an obvious
    doppelganger

an obstruction, a defeat, a cracked crucible

mechanical beyond a compassionate clause

language of the industrial chorus

duplication and duplication ad infinitum

and not the dread taught by *Frankenstein* or *The Time Machine*.
Run without looking, the thrill of icy wind on our skin

I like a good change of regimen myself, after all, there are
    some traditions
that need to be refreshed, replaced or abolished

Hope or 'whatever' depends upon a certain ignorance
    of history
and an ability to close your eyes, concentrate
    on the cold rush and not the fall

Theoretically, anything we build can be dismantled even if
    it takes twice as long
and nothing can be proven after we're gone except
    what we know already

He said, 'Science is not the same as technology, although both
have become dependent upon dollars' so that nothing is
    for the sake of curiosity

as history teaches us is necessary, besides we like to play
    with our food
as we have learned is a characteristic of ape descendants,
    not to mention

a suicidal tendency. *The animal eye sees with wonderful accuracy*
the wonder of the great abyss

DAYDREAMERS INVESTIGATE MORALITY

We live, roughly speaking, in the last generation of human beings …
– Whitfield Diffie, Sun Microsystems

There is no theoretical limit to the human life span
People can just keep repairing themselves

Insert coded messages into the genes of bacteria
The mode by which the Earth will die

Have no illusions
How much money do you have?

The notion of death as something that arrived by accident
Create an explosion on aging

It shouldn't be allowed he says
What the heck was he talking about?

Ignore the possibility that defeating death
is not a fundamentally good thing to do

In the business plan
death is an impediment to sales

In the forever plan
how will we navigate the interminable?

To come this far in human life
To the unflinching face of the end.

GEONOME SEQUENCE

What would we know of a person
if we were given their precise geographical coordinates?

If their genomic data
was solidified into a statue?

The garment of the body is a dialogue
impressive sculptural shapes directly from sound

Fantasy relies on re-describing,
exposing our own blind spots

Invisible forces construct form
morphing is then reversed

Vivid colors are a powerful tool
that inflate and unfold

The body metamorphosed through an artificial man-made
force remote controlled fiberglass

where heat is used to modify magnetism and erosion
threshold of the end of consciousness

The shady territory between realism and surrealism
The project of preserving the end of the world

the intricate codes of the body
before minus now

new identities can be clothed
biometric analyses of chromosomes and stresses

a new anthropology of the isolated

KATHRYN KERR

Kathryn Kerr was born in St Louis, MO, during a thunderstorm at the end of World War II, and grew up on a farm in southern Illinois. She has worked in libraries and archives, as a photographer, a field botanist and an editor. An MFA program at Southern Illinois University drew her into Irish Studies. Though she has retired from full-time teaching, she reads, writes and volunteers at the local history museum. She has published numerous articles, essays and poems, including four chapbooks of poetry: *Coneflower, Equinox, First Frost* and *Turtles All the Way Down.*

RIVERS

Born by the Mississippi,
a flow like sorghum
like Southern Comfort,
smooth opaque surface,
strong undertow,
a river of gars and 'gators,
sometimes a rampage
pulling down gallery forests,
grain bins, coops full of hens.

Grew up by the Cache
which slides down from hills
to meander through old ox-bows,
cypress and tupelo, sleeping
in the old Ohio's bed,
spreading brown skirts
to draw down ducks in winter.

Lived by Indian Creek
and Big Muddy, slow rivers
sometimes rising up to steal
a field of freshly planted oats
or mosey through acres
of ripened corn.

And now this Corrib
sings, swirls and dances,
kicking up lacy white
underskirts, a ceili,
she rises and falls,
flings herself coldly
over stone into ocean.

RECOGNITION
for St Columba

Columba, I met an Irishman
who recalls living your life
on the cold seaweed strewn strand
of western Ireland. He knew
your words before he read them,
knew them in his own hot heart.

And I knew him when I saw in his eyes
the medieval streets of Galway
when fall afternoon sun
strikes grey stones at a late angle.
When I was there, remembering,
I searched, but knew no one.
Still, the old church, St. Nicholas,
for the preserver of sailors, was familiar.

'Sister Poet' Columba called me.
Somewhere on the windy western edge
there must have been a weaver,
now unknown, unnamed, who knew
the hermit, who shared the warmth
of her peat fire on stormy nights,
who learned from him fasting and verse,
who taught him plants and spells.

KINTSUGI
(the art of repairing broken pottery with lacquer dusted or mixed with gold)

Start with the chicken pox scars
they are faint, now, but visible
on my nose and chin.

The scar on my left knuckle, gone,
but the top of my right foot
and my left shin are marred.

I suppose stretch marks count?
My first daughter left them only
under my belly button,

but the second daughter
scarred me from ribs down,
even behind. All small,

I'll be veined with gold.
But take off my bra –
you'll find the large scar

has faded, but part is absent.
More is missing in my axilla.
The hole punched in my side –

I can't see it, but I find it
with my fingers. These will
take quite a bit of gold.

Repaired, I'm quite valuable,
unless, of course, you prefer
a vessel never broken.

A GARDEN PEACH,

soft yellow, almost fuzzy, flattened globe lies within my
palm, last year my favorite tomato. Its mild sweetness
replaced in my affection the Cherokee Purples whose
purely deep flavor I had favored. Last winter I told my
brother of them, my brother liked Big Boys for their bright
color and generous size. I praised Cherokee Purples, not too
pretty, but with a strong color and flavor; the sweet, small,
green striped Russian Zebra tomatoes, bred for a cooler
climate; but best of all the Garden Peach, whose soft
sweetness was as tempting as Eden's fruit. I wanted Jim to
come to my city's farmer's market and see the tomatoes in
their little green quart boxes, an arrangement of yellow,
orange, red, purple, green like a candy store. I could see in
his eyes that frivolity compared to the bushels he brought in
for canning, big tomatoes, red skins gleaming.

Now I hold this Garden Peach in my palm and smell it. Jim
died before his tomatoes ripened. And I hope where he is
there are lots of big, red tomatoes. Lord knows, I've lost my
taste for this little yellow one.

If a late June afternoon
humid with clover hay, just cut,
and honeysuckle spills
pheromones, while shadows
soften as sunlight slopes
through thick air –

If that moment could be tasted
six months later when frost
tries to pry the panes from frames
of the windows, sweaters spark
in indoor air, and cats cower
from the zap of touch –

If that taste could be cooled,
kept, and rolled thick and gold
over my hot tongue, along edge
of sensitive teeth, leaving
lips sticky. That thickness –
taste of remembered desire.

CHORAL MUSIC

Singing closely together, they don't see each other, but hear
each voice as part their own. Breathing together, they
become one being, enmeshed in the reticulate sounds. When
breath unites, heartbeats synchronize, one body coalesces
from individual voices, the way Fuligo's invisible cells,
scattered along the tree bark, one day hear a chemical note
that brings them together, coalescing, one golden body
rising, harmonious cells singing together.

APRIL LEO

'enough confusion in April to send you on a pointless journey
or to convince you to get a tattoo from an artist who can't spell',
my horoscope warns. Oh, Hell. That was March. I want to know
certainty now, not swim both directions, again this month.

Life has no revisions, I know, and no rehearsals.
I played a role in a drama that I had not read the script for,
just handed the part as I walked on stage and had to
improvise. I want to say it was a role I wasn't meant for.

I don't know still if that was just a walk on, a bit part,
or if it was a tryout and I might get a callback.
I don't even know if I should take that role if offered.
Maybe I'll just go get a tattoo.

KATHRYN KIRKPATRICK

Kathryn Kirkpatrick is Professor of English at Appalachian State University where she teaches environmental literature, animal studies and Irish Studies and co-coordinates the Animal Studies minor. She is the author of seven books of poetry, including collections addressing climate change, human illness and non-human animals – *Unaccountable Weather* (2011) and *Our Held Animal Breath* (2012). *The Fisher Queen: New & Selected Poems*, was published in 2019 by Salmon Press. Kirkpatrick is the editor of *Border Crossings: Irish Women Writers and National Identities* (U of Alabama Press, 2000) and co-editor with Borbala Farago of *Animals in Irish Literature and Culture* (Palgrave, 2015).

VISITATION

A crow, enormous, lights
on my left hand, not painful
but powerful and insistent,
as I drive and drive, my mother
in tow beside me. *Okay,*
I'll pay attention, I say,
to placate the crow, hard
to steer, to stay on the road
with such a weight of otherworldly
freight, and who can say if it's guidance
I'm getting, a warning, a visitation,
as if that crow found me a priority
and Ted Hughes himself sent her
even though it's me having done
so little for any crow in particular.
My mother finds the dream ordinary
because she knows such birds by name,
is often visited by rose-breasted grosbeaks,

but when the crow dreams
what need has she of me?
With her wing of blue black,
her sharp eye of dark, she
follows rhythms we do not see,
with us as the air is with us,
as I am with my mother, guiding who
guided me, feathers of memory,
words in the blue black, so that
I am homed and homing, while the crow
waits for the walnut under the wheel
to shatter for her ready beak,
and what a shrewd flight she
makes of it, dreaming our head-tops
from above, our need of direction,
our useful tire at the intersection,

and love with its earthbound claw,
need with its open wings.

THIS WEATHER

Because I don't have much time
she writes to a sitting president
asking for legislation to cool
the world down, a brief, lopsided

scrawl, but pointed, *I'm 83 years old,*
the essential coming through
like headlights in fog, a lucid
assessment I hadn't imagined,

telling him, but also telling me.
I stop behind my taking care
smile, her gentle indirection more
than I'm prepared to meet. She knows

full well what we've not yet said.
Please get busy. I don't have much
time left. So much at stake alongside
this weather, this whether or not

I can find the words. Of course, she's
the one with the trouble, only not today,
as she turns her half blind eyes
to me like a majestic bird, some wild

intelligence from the middle brain assessing.
You look sad, from the land of apparently
impaired memory. *Is it because I said*
I don't have much time left?

THE BATH

Insufficient splashing and you'd
call, as if I'd long gone under.
What did you say? *Are you okay?*

I'd make a wave or two, sufficient
to be heard alive, and to this
day I'm not sure if I'd wake and

catch myself in time, drifting off.
I fall asleep, then startle in
warm water, or groggy, lift

awake, away from full immersion
as when at night, the memories
come on, and I'm awash again

in grief, not your absence so much
as your going, the last laps,
you making a clean start each

living day, up for it, the past
washed clear away. I wanted you
bathed in lavender and rose, your

going only a matter of
easing toward the last warm shore, not
the porcelain edge, the hard fall

when I wasn't there to catch you.

only days after – her dying – her death, me threading back
– through the bruises and falls – the calls I made – and
didn't make, grief – winding me – tight with the should –
have dones, mother spoke – to me through the – basswood
tree, down in the side yard – that morning a soft – rot of
wood – a shock of fissured – branches – the ground –
covered in a mat of cross-hatched – twigs and larger –
silver slivered strands – I stood – transfixed, the ordinary –
fallen away, she – gave me her brokenness – there, the
slow years – of breaking I wept – knew what she'd – said I
don't mean I – tried for meaning, I – mean it was – there,
before me, how – death undoes the – world, her now – in
it, hundreds of broken – twigs I gathered – up in baskets,
they – started small – fires all winter and – start them still I
– want to say they – start a fire in me

TURKEY FEATHER

1

hollow at the center a many
stranded soft rough-sided
oblong halved by a quill
once attached to the body
of a bird how does the quill
attach how loosen how grow
from a dense body hollow
packed tight with other
feathers and how fall there
at my feet and now in my hand
after so many living years

2

to say I am stranded
like a feather lost from
the body of a bird to say
it is like the soft and rough
of family that bisecting
hollow quill how I keep trying
to take that feather for me
but it makes its way back
to the body of the bird
now flown and I am left
holding the fawn-tipped
part of her

TURBULENCE

Of the stomach lifting. Of the weightless
where I was and am again variety.

Sway and crack, our craft. Slalom
the wind. So much carbon in the currents.

Of the climate kind. Of the jerk and thwack.
Of the hurtling toward. Shake right out

of our human. As if we might not
settle back into these bodies,

but land instead in someone else.
Yet the hare far below isn't empty

to receive us. Neither is the horse.
They have their own embodied plans.

We will have to settle beside ourselves
blurred boundaries and all. Bump,

rattle, and creak. Our enlightened selves
grasp cokes, play solitaire, read, sleep,

going on as if what's happening isn't.

JOSEPH LENNON

Joseph Lennon is the Emily C. Riley Director of the Center for Irish Studies and Associate Dean in the College of Liberal Arts and Sciences at Villanova University, and Professor of English. He writes on Irish and Indian literature and culture and has published poetry in journals such as *Poetry Ireland*, *New Hibernia Review*, *Denver Quarterly*, and *Natural Bridge*. His first book of poems, *Fell Hunger*, was published by Salmon Poetry.

ENSKY

Eyes appear
to see one another.

Poetry is an old woman
sitting on a trunk

of driftwood facing land;
the ocean fans behind her.

She rests as clouds do,
upon the sky, so clear of pressure.

She seems an image
a gaze you cannot meet,

until you realize it is you
averting your sight.

You follow her expression
as swells cap white at sea.

When your eyes meet, her face
comes close, her crow's feet

narrow, green irises widen,
and lashes flower.

BROKEN IN

The car window lay
Spattered – glittering like scales
on a fishcutter's apron –

across a seat where the books
had been, so I spent the morning
beachcombing empty lots
and plots for them.

A heavy net at night always
feels a good catch, but books
by Blasket Islanders
about a now empty island
may be impossible to fence.

Cops think kids had a spree –
ten cars burgled, a circular saw
swiped; I recognize thieves
by the dart of their eyes,
glances moving to hide
what's left to lose.

When young, a friend stole
a stereo from a remote tower,
and we went back for more –
we smashed a window before
a siren felled us in its waves –
we ditched our tools, splashed
the yard, vanished in corn rows.

When I hit the river, I took it
to the tracks that led home –
every set of lights oncoming,
a cop splaying night with a beam,
panning for eyes or legs dashing –

then eased over the trestle in town,
as cars sailed through green washes
or floated in the stoplight.

I imagined county cops shifting
weight in our kitchen, leg to leg,
finger-ringing cuffs, questioning,
waiting for me – if not, my folks
would be up pacing, phoning, but
when I got home, there was no one –
sirens never heard,
the house gone half
strange or stolen or not my own.

THROWN OVER
for J and J

I

When Fergus, spine broken,
held his fiancée, Anne, he braced her
until she burst their home;

when Justin slipped the cinching knot
the night before the wedding,
he finally fell free;

when Johanna sat in a Brooklyn chair,
darkly, pulling split-ends,
I slipped through the key hole.

We're still wearing
the gilt livery, looped and knotted,
from service to the damaged.

II

The poet came down the mountain
with hard news: 'for days I
lay unconscious on the floor' –

a 100-year hurricane had hit the coast.
The party shut down, the wine corked,
the fig cakes collapsed.

'Now I know', she intoned, 'our children grow up,
with compasses that don't show our Sargassos.
No pulleys nor maths nor cranes

nor ropes for righting listing ships
can help after rocks are struck.
Risk management, a bent nail for builders'.

III

Our fathers unscrewed
our belly buttons,
to show us how we fall apart.

Ophelia gathered flowers
for an uncertain end, her beau lost,
Laertes left staring at his hands.

Interrupted songs, broken lines
might converge in art,
as dancers stretch for balance,

as painters shadow distance,
but we can't straighten out others –
the ones uncombed by their mothers.

IV

They say the ships wrecked
on Kerry shores
threw survivors on sand,

gasping, to walk the strand
for their jetsam –
gathered by islanders

who hauled their canvases from waves,
lifted boards and crates of tea
to steep over fire,

to drink and dye together –
to bury the drowned,
to sew new sails.

16 October 2017, Dublin

KERRY SONG

Time has went, time beyond,
Love has sung, so and on.

Mountains through windows,
Days are spent, lived no matter,

Mountains of butter, curling
In the hotel, silks of songs curtailed,

A dummy piano, far from tuned
Sits in the foyer, painted shut

Yet opens by the gingery
Fingers of boys, reviving

Unmoored promises
Of lovers, of keys, of hours like this.

Time has went, time beyond,
Love so sings, on and on.

JAMES LIDDY

James Liddy was born in Dublin in 1934, raised in Coolgreany, County Wexford, and educated at UCD and King's Inns. His books include *Blue Mountain, Corca Bascinn, Baudelaire's Bar Flowers, Collected Poems* and *Gold Set Dancing*. For many years he was a Professor in the English Department at the University of Wisconsin-Milwaukee where he taught creative writing and Irish and Beat literature. Arlen House published Brian Arkins' *James Liddy: A Critical Study* in 2001. James Liddy died at his home in the United States in 2008.

A COBALT BLUE VALENTINE

The Angel Gabriel glides
in by the window
wearing hand-me-
down wings to disorientate
a maiden pure:
pure truth to be mixed with wine.

'Hello, darling,
someone has sent me
to make you sigh and tremble
because you shall
lay out a child
whose bones muscles
skin veins articulate
a palace of cobalt blue without extinction'.

'I know no man – how can I do this?'

'We have all known angels'.

Lovely edifice
body made with light.
Gabriel's blaze
is a huge torch
while his white hot heart
dives down to become a penis
must dance
through the leaves of her tree.

Mary's deeper color
cobalt blue.

Yes, dramatically we are all
Virgin Marys confused between yes and no,
ordered around by negatives and positives.

Advised by ourselves badly, worse
advised by our culture
say in Middle School.
Note, love is mandatory
and enforced by angel corps.

Back to the kid now
flesh and blood's consciousness
what name do you want:
Jesus Mohammed Francis
or maybe Arthur Rimbaud?
The event happens in Ethiopia
the day warm the carafe of wine
on the window sill half drunk.

2000

THE EMPEROR'S BODYGUARD IS HIS BODY

In spring the emperor wears
a T-shirt and a bird cage

At Easter the emperor
only displays a pretty bonnet

In summer the emperor
takes out a Byzantium fig leaf

Autumn the emperor
is too love-sick to walk out

At Halloween the emperor's
concession is a hair-do

Winter the emperor orders
unneeded heavy sports jackets

Thanksgiving the emperor
wants a cloth on the table

New Year's Eve the emperor
says no one should bring garments

On St. Valentine's the emperor
puts on clothes worn by pedophiles

In the dawning of the day
the Faerie Queen with but a crown

The only Emperor is the
one who wears no clothes
while eating ice cream

2001

A PROFESSOR'S CHRISTMAS

I listen to music in bed, that's the night mind,
Christmas, I thought, mother's not around
then there will be no real drinking.

The dead drive around in my bed-night mind
sometimes they rent cars occasionally they buy them.

I have been led around by the spirit
but have had long drinks with the demon
who shows my students campuses on the coasts,
bow down by ivy league ocean or lake
you shall gain extensive tuition relief.

Shall the righteous ever have a change of heart,
I pine for melody and there's mediocrity
departmental politics at the heart of gender politics,
I like the student who is nuts about baseball
or the one who sings Morrissey and Smith songs.

Gregorian chant liberates, it makes me
think of mother doing real drinking.

I am the mother and father of bachelor parties
the Beatitudes are for Bohemians
and it doesn't bother me there is a mother
in Christianity but no wife.

Lying here I thought of all the Christmases
before there were Christmas trees
and all the presents with no set place to lay them,
I thought of the Masses before there were Malls
and I heard in whatever was being sung on the radio
the possibility of priests rerouting needs:

Christ's image sings at the end of the bed
with the plausibility of what Eric says tonight
in the County Clare doesn't exist, love.
Luke 5.29

2001

THE LORD'S PRAYER

I

When I was young I remember people being admitted to
hospital for 'exhaustion', the wonderful not woeful faces of
sweethearts mesmerized into social occasions. In the
exclusion of our exhaustion.

II

Snow drifts impede attempts to repeat words.

III

The Prayer sentences, our consciousness not our elation. I
can't compose any stillness. Also I can't turn my palms
out, that was for Clare who has died; I can't hold hands in
the pews, that's for the night. What I know of evil: it's not
knowing what you're doing after a certain age.

IV

Cunningham talks about 'epiousios' (not found anywhere
else in Greek), 'daily'. Day today is a tax on the
extraordinary yet the table is made for bread.

V

All wreaths (and wine) ask forgiveness.

VI

Simone Weil's exhausted commentary on the Greek text.
He is present in person. She recited it in the morning, 'The
very first words tear my thoughts from my body and
transport them to a place outside space ...'

VII

Serious fatigue. Maybe try.

Christmas 2002

DAVID LLOYD

David Lloyd is the author of ten books. His fiction includes a novel, *Over the Line* (Syracuse University Press, 2013) and two story collections, *Boys: Stories and a Novella* (Syracuse University Press, 2004) and *The Moving of the Water* (SUNY Press, 2018). His poetry collections include *Warriors* (Salt Publishing, 2012), *The Gospel According to Frank* (New American Press, 2009), and *The Everyday Apocalypse* (Three Conditions Press, 2002). In 2000, he received the Poetry Society of America's Robert H. Winner Memorial Award. He directs the Creative Writing Program at Le Moyne College in Syracuse, NY.

WARP-SPASM

One night Peter met Ava for drinks at the Luau
where someone saw them being seen

by everyone who's anyone, except Frank,
and the someone told Louella Parsons,

who told her readers who told each other
news already old the next morning.

Where's Frank in all of this? Frank asked himself,
so sorry at the death of love, the insubstantial treason,

the post-mortem of an illusion once world-renowned.
But rage, rage, thank God, is its own reward,

before, during, and after; that pulse of life
coiled like a vicious jack-in-the-box,

its lid perpetually about to pop
and release into the world the screaming head.

It takes a lifetime of practice to get it right.
It takes a self large as a skyscraper.

Muscles tense, brow furrows, teeth grind,
testicles swell ten times their size, pores leak,

eyes swivel in their sockets, hairs like bayonets,
bourbon sucked down by the quart.

Ready, at last. Two in the morning
on the phone to Peter: *What the fuck*

you doing with Ava?
You want both your legs broken?

Rage and release. Rage and release.
So good to be alive.

Frank Sinatra read gossip columnist Louella Parsons' report that
Peter Lawford had been spotted at a Beverly Hills restaurant having
drinks with Ava Gardner.

'*Warp-Spasm*': the frenzy that Cúchulainn, hero of the *Táin Bó
Cúailnge*, experiences before battle.

'Warp-Spasm' was published in *The Gospel According to Frank*: New
American Press, 2009.

SELF-PORTRAITS WITHOUT A MIRROR

1. Superman

Who made it? When? Why?
To keep me in, or others out?

No matter, my ramparts repel the atomic blast
of my father's disused pipe, the tsunami

of my mother's hymns from the kitchen,
the crawl of teachers' lava boiling

to my doorstep, a brother's flinging
of bodies over the parapets

with messages carved on the chests:
who do you think you are? what do you think you are?

Girls that will not speak, tunnel their faces
into my dreams.

A battering ram of knuckles
punches the front gate.

Middle-aged archers aim arrows
at my armored heart, my helmeted head.

Ladders of love touch my bulwarks.
Starve me. Thirst me.

Pinch me. Need me. Feel my smooth stone.
Catapult your every word toward me.

But against solitude's fortress – what hope?
I scream. I pray. I text myself –

Break through with meat, with drink!
With reinforcements of me! –

But I cannot muster.
The walls are too stout, mortared

with my blood, my flesh.

2. Cinderella

Magic is an act of will.
No matter the shape of a foot,
the size of a slipper.

I will not sweep those ashes.
I will not scrub that pot.

To love a man is an act of will.
He might be a brute.
He might be a dunce.
But I will dance, palm on his epaulet,
fingers on his back, caressing skin
beneath princely fabric as we glide
the polished floor. Magic. Magic.
Mahogany and gold.

Is it willful? Is it strange?
Heat in the cheeks, lick of a lip.
I stare into his eyes, as steady as a tablecloth.

I will not trip on the curving staircase.
I will not squat in the closet when he knocks.

In the carriage, racing to the palace,
steam pumping from horses' black nostrils,
I will not glance back at my weeping sisters

or down at the smear of blood
on glass, my foot an exact fit.

3. *Dracula*

Sometimes we just need
to suck the blood of a virgin
on a balcony, beneath a full moon,
with rabid bats circling

and angry villagers on the march.
I'm not proud of my needs
any more than I'm proud of my ageless age
or the European cut of my suit.

But I'm proud of these teeth, sharp and scrubbed
like cutlery on a set table.
My what big teeth you have, she whispers
when I open for air.

I need a throat the color of the moon.
I need the inside gift, always-flowing.
It's my birthday, I say. *The day of get.*
Shall I unwrap you?

And she lifts fingers to my pale cheek –
half-closes her eyes. But wait, wait:
are those eyelids swollen?
Is that nail on her thumb too thick?

The down on her arm too dark?
Is need a disease?
And is she contagious?

Strange how the small is huge in memory.
Like the Grand Union where I biked as a boy
to see unearthly lobsters in sea-green
tanks and a row of gumball machines as big
as basketballs. Strange how distances
expand for the lost one with a found need

to reach home – and strange how home and need
themselves make huge the beloved in memory:
a father, a mother, pure distances
as near as the wounded girl or boy
you were. They needed to see you grow big,
didn't they? – each year measuring your green

shoot of a self with marks on a wall – a green
that lengthens and darkens. There's no greater need
than the measuring hand of a father, bigger
than fear, big as a mother's memory
of carrying for heavy months her boy,
walking away now, keeping his distance –

measuring marks on his own wall: distance
from the first home, first church, his father's green
thumb working the first garden, where the boy
planted a sunflower seed because it needs,
he thought, almost nothing. In memory
it shot up like Jack's fairytale stalk – biggest

bedtime story become the biggest
flower-head, the newest sun. Yes, distances
are untrue; mutating in memory –
lobster tanks that one year are sea-green,
are earth-brown the next because we need
our needs more than facts. I was a boy

when the world was almost as fast as a boy
could run and nearly as close and as big
as air. Where was home? What did I need?
Gumball machines. Unearthly lobsters. Distant
suns. Mother carrying. Father's green
thumb, gone too early. What is memory

but how a boy-become-a-man measures distance?
So, measure: a bike, a big story, a green
thumb, a first home, a need: a memory.

ED MADDEN

Ed Madden is professor of English and director of Women's and Gender Studies at the University of South Carolina. He is the author of four books of poetry, most recently *Ark*. His poems have appeared in *Crazyhorse, Prairie Schooner, Poetry Ireland Review* as well as in *Best New Poets 2007, The Book of Irish American Poetry* and *Hard Lines: Rough South Poetry*. He was a 2010 research fellow at NUI Galway and the 2017 Neenan Research Fellow at Boston College Ireland in Dublin. In 2015, he was named the inaugural poet laureate for Columbia, South Carolina.

SHAME

No one picks up. The telephone line is silent.

Home for a funeral, and my mother says:
You know deep down you're really ashamed.

And I am ashamed, because she says so.
The house is swaddled in darkness and shame,

dark carols of shame sweep the fields.

A cold wind clears the cemetery, but shame
is the muffler around my neck, the gloves on my hands.

Shame is a web. I am an insect, stuck in it.
Or I keep it around me, spittlebug, cocoon.

The airplane can't lift up enough
to get beyond the layers of stratus and shame.

I drag it back with me – yep, there
on the conveyor with the other luggage.

Sometimes, when no one is watching,
I take a handful and swallow it, so sweet.

It's coming up now all around the house,
the bright green blades of it, the flowers.

FROSTWORK

December, and a scrim of frost
glistened on the window,
the morning a glaze of light and ice.

We didn't know what we didn't know.

The lawn crunched beneath our boots like snow,
the brown grass a frozen thatch.

Last day before the winter break.
It was fourth grade, and my first glasses
fogging up on the bus.

I couldn't see, and then I could.

His Shirt

was sweat-soaked, smoke-
threaded, Salem packet pocketed –

the carton on the dash or behind
the truck's seat – warm-water-

washed with boot-cut jeans
patched with grease, and thick

boot socks heeled and toed
grey, silver rivets for buttons,

studded up the placket and cuffs –
fit me well enough,

though he was smaller than me
by then.

November, the Bees

Bees cling to the frostweed's gold flowers –

the long stem bends with them – pinned
there by the cold, the rain, stuck

by the persistence of last hungers –

the way my dad would eat anything sweet,
those last weeks, those last days.

THE ANGEL OF HISTORY

I dig up the iris, lift corms crammed thirty years thick
and barely blooming

near the road, make some room. The yard
is cobbled with rotten acorns –

my brother shovels them up, fills the wheelbarrow,
throws them on the fire –

all those possibles pop and hiss, each rotten the same way.
My mom turns in her sleep, an angel

still reaching for the ruins. It's not that words can be taken
back, no, but now we're saying now we're trying to say now

we're trying to say it different,

and there are five buckets of iris left over.
My aunt wants some, my cousins, some for the graveyard,

where they'll bloom after it's all over, after
my dad's gone. Somewhere

everything happens all at once: He turns away, he turns
back. I leave, I return.

THRESHING
for Bert, after Ruth 3

The last truck is filled with grain, the sun
is a dull coal at the end of the rows.
The combines cough and fall still. It's cold.
I grab my dad's jacket from the truck, pull it on.
His cigarette's a small flame in the dark.
Across the river, the man I will meet
is a boy fidgeting a box of sweets,
sitting beside his mom in a country store,
doing as he's told. Too kind to debtors,
someday she will lose the store. Tomorrow
we'll burn the fields, the stubbled rows.
The sky is dark and empty. Across the river,
the man I will meet is still a boy who does not
know me. I button up my dad's jacket,
finger a measure of grain in the pocket.
The men talk, words scattered like chaff.
The fields will blacken with flame and ash.
The man I will meet is years from now.

MARY MADEC

Mary Madec's work has appeared most recently in *Reading the Future: New Writing from Ireland,* (Arlen House, 2018), *The Interpreter's House, The Irish Times* (1/4/2017), *Stand* (Autumn 2016, Autumn 2018), *The Cork Literary Review* (Commemorative Issue, Autumn 2016), the international anthology *The Poets' Quest for God* (Eyewear, 2016), *Washing Windows? Irish Women Write Poetry* (Arlen House, 2016) and *Even The Daybreak* (Salmon, 2016). In 2008 she won the Hennessy XO Award for Emerging Poetry. Her third book *The Egret Lands With News From Other Parts* is due from Salmon in spring 2019.

THE PINK DANCING COSTUME
for Medbh McGuckian

I shall have no check to my genius from beginning to end.
In marriage, the man is supposed to provide for the woman,
the woman to make the home agreeable to the man;
he is to purvey, and she is to smile.

But in dancing, their duties are exchanged; he smiles
agreable to the game, while she furnishes the fan, the
    lavender water.
a perception of duties in a former age for another place,
the conditions today incapable of comparison.

I fill the tracings of the dragon with stem stitch, the silk threads
lined up in every inch of his long body, laid out on the great
    circle
of my bishop's pink with its black satin lining, its fine crochet
white rose collar and cuffs. I work steadily with my mother

until it is done and I stand in front of her as if to walk
    upon the stage,
the light jumping on the silken threads, my feet pointed
    until the pounce
for the start of the music, turns and twirls and rocks in the dance
of the nation, the magic of my feet, the pride and elation of
    our handiwork:

One two three four, one two three four, one two three four,
    up and down
One two three four, one two three four, one two three four, up
    and down
Hop to three four, cross two three four, one tip one, rock two
    three,
Hop to three four, cross two three four, one tip one, rock two
    three ...

THE GREEN ROOM

We, the women, come and go,
not one common lingo between us

as we sit, sip tea or coke,
too self-absorbed to do the crossword
before our turn to walk out into the limelight,

the old fears at us, as if we are back in the classroom
pitched against each other
wondering who has the sweetest voice.

We were, are, never in the boys' club
though some of us are lifted up like oracles
for our prophecies, the aptness of our words.

Here we are polite, deferent, as at *Poetry Ireland Introductions*.
We stretch our fingers to take Boland's biscuits from a plate
with a doily in the centre of the table, savour the delicate taste.

We think of the clues: One dreams of a horse with a mane sent
from across the bitter sea looking in over the half door
at the cream crawling up the jug.

An office girl rubs Lincoln creams from her mouth,
counts pages offshore, longing for the boat
back to Dun Laoighaire.

In Galway, an abandoned nest keeps its place in an old ruin
miles from Donegal, a silk road wends its way to a sea wall
where a woman plunges a knife in the wave.

Somewhere in Belfast a young mother looks through a window
over Strangford Lough and an older woman
searches for patchwork pieces on the internet

and all over the island the interpolation of Greek lament in
    timid voices
of the lineage. I am checking out words in the Dictionary
of Obscure Sorrows, finding one word that fits all,

monochopsis, *the subtle but persistent feeling of being maladapted,*
for example, a selkie on a beach, – *lumbering, clumsy,*
easily distracted but pretending not to be

huddled in the company of other misfits, you recognize this
your voice one scale at least above *the ambient roar*
of your intended habitat,

in which you'd be fluidly, brilliantly, effortlessly at home,
if only they would listen. Get them to listen, all of them,
you tell yourself, as you make your way from the Green Room.

She wants to know why girls begin with *g* boys with *b*? I
measure in the tunnels of my thought possible links tease,
guh, 'girl' and *beh,* 'boy' against *guh,* 'good' and *beh,* 'bad'
by which time she's had another question. I think of how
questions hold onto us like ivy on trees, encircle our
certainties. I tell her we are trees, listening to the code of
other leaves, poplars trembling, sycamores swaying,
willows swishing in the mystery of the breeze, in each a
purling through xylem and phloem, carrrying riffs of
thrush, caw of crow into our core. She wonders about
sounds whose meaning we do not know? Our questions
hold us, I say as we stretch our arms to the big sky, light
and air, moving through blue then grey, our ears straining
for even the littlest sigh, every sound registered, even
before it has meaning, *Could you hear that leaf fall?* she asks
as we watch the first autmn leaves make their way to the
ground. Before I can even answer she has found in a tangle
of ivy a magic home in a Cypress bole, *Please, please can we
play house!* Whose woods these are I think I know. We sip
rainwater tea from big leaves and eat wildgrass cookies
and, before we go, we hug the rough unyielding bark to
say thankyou. *Can we come tomorrow again? And the day
after? And the day after?* she says *And then the tree will know
what we sound like and say hello!*

Cobalt gentians at Eagle's Rock with their startling white eyes
and out across the Burren, orchid spikes
of pink and white and bird's-foot trefoil and burnet rose
and the common violet and all that grows
softly moving in the low breeze close to the ground,
in among rock and grass as dry as desert scutch.
You are asking yourself what compels you as such,
you, with your great consciousness compared to theirs
hacking out survival in the hardest layers
of rock, what is it you need of their perfection and fragility?
As you gaze on the delicate petals a certain equanimity
comes, which leaves you searching still for what precisely occurs
in you, as you flit over the velvet blue, satin yellow, pink
    and white lace
and burst for their beauty, resilience, grace.

No, I Cannot Go Home, I Don't Know What To Say To The Children

We drive through the housing estates of South Dublin,
flowering trees sodden with tears

I imagine pristine lives unstained by words such as I
    would have to utter,
so we drive for over an hour

until the rain stops or the flood recedes or whatever it was
    that opened
a path back to our house. I turn the key

and go quietly in from the night
the baby still holding court in his chair
until he sees me, wants to be picked up.

My older son, flitting his dark eyes
to finds words to ask us, then asks what
we brought home for him.

The babysitter hurries away says *we'll talk tomorrow*
and now it's snacks and stories and hugs
and no ugly words are spoken and when they are tucked

the memory of the doctor crestfallen
delivering this news to the young woman
of thirty three, who is me.

The soft breathing of my sleeping children
rises and falls into the silence as I lie awake
wondering still, not knowing what to say.

AMPHITRITE AT ACHILL HEAD

On the one side are overshadowing rocks against which dash the
mighty billows of the Amphitrite, the goddess of blue-glancing seas
– Homer, *Odyssey* 12. 60 ff.

I watch her rise in this Achill woman's eyes
something homey and fragile about her as she sips
opposite me, as if her tea were full of essential plankton,
as if her bulging eyes were the result of hard earned insights.

I see her survey the sound, imagine her out there,
her hair in tresses, gathered in a net, the colour of yellow
    flag iris.
Once she was slender and exquisite as a birch tree,
now she is heavy and beaten by south westerlies.

Often she skipped along the road in Kildavnet
tells me as she remembers it, smiles, clear as she does,
what she once was. She doesn't tell me about Dympna
or why she died.

Her fish eyes scan Achill head
the thick though tender lips of her cavernous mouth open
and close for sips of the sea, she knows how to live there
proceeds unperturbed through her playground,

her tail and fins at work go gently into unfamiliar territory,
make deep forays into places no one else would go
as she weaves her old ways through the current
and when she sets out to the deep

she trembles with love for the silver shoals
released beyond the tombolo, her heart wrenched from
what she knows as she watches them with envy and resignation
rise like foals from the spray,
released to the world,
galloping to that destiny ahead of them.

IGGY MCGOVERN

Iggy McGovern is Fellow Emeritus in the School of Physics at Trinity College Dublin. He has published three collections of poetry with Dedalus Press: *The King of Suburbia* (2005), *Safe House* (2010) and *The Eyes of Isaac Newton* (2017). *A Mystic Dream of 4*, a poetic biography of William Rowan Hamilton, 19th-century Irish mathematician and poet, is published by Quaternia Press (2013). He edited the anthology *20|12: Twenty Irish Poets Respond to Science in Twelve Lines* (Dedalus Press, 2012). Awards include the Ireland Chair of Poetry Bursary, the Glen Dimplex New Writers Award for Poetry and the Hennessy Literary Award.

'LIKE SOLDER WEEPING OFF THE SOLDERING IRON'
i.m. Gus McEvoy

Reading the Heaney poem that begins:
'When all the others were away at Mass'
the fourth line (here as title) prompts a grin
to see you now through memory's looking glass:

As if it were a piece of art nouveau,
the floor was silver speckled round your chair
with solder splashes from the steady flow
of students seeking radio repairs.

The Coleraine campus backed onto The Bann
as if determined to keep facing East;
some might have tagged our lab 'The Vatican'
'Two Catholics, and one of them's a priest!'

An early start to say Mass at first light,
your days were given to experiments
then evenings in pursuit of Civil Rights,
so these were not competing elements.

Forgive my adding one more jigsaw piece.
McDonagh* neatly caught it plosively:
Life seen through all or any of four P's:
Prayer, Physics, Politics and Poetry.

* *Rev. Enda McDonagh, Professor of Moral Theology and Canon Law*

TRAVELS WITH MY UNCLE
i.m. Tommy-Thomas-Oweny McGovern

When you boarded the through train in '21
were you even aware of the self-serving seal
that was struck for the *Sligo, Leitrim & Northern
Counties Railway Company* showing
two steam locomotives colliding, of which
one was derailed while the other remained
on its track – the seal meant to celebrate
the hard-won success in reaching Sligo
ahead of its rival, now gone to the wall?
No matter, from Belcoo to Enniskillen
and *The Great Northern* train to Londonderry
to board the *Columbia* emigrant ship
just like your two older sisters before you,
bound for New York, New York.

Forty years on, I'm allowed on my own
to retrace the path of your last railway journey,
but all of those trains have long since departed:
it's a bus to Omagh, change for Enniskillen,
where we pick up the C.I.E. one to Sligo;
sit tight at Belcoo, for soon we're all out
while a Customs Official paces the aisle,
checking for items self-styled duty-free,
policing a border that you never knew:
Now we're in Eire, The Free State, Blacklion,
we sit in *The Bush Bar*, and nurse a *Cidona*
till sometime or other, a cousin remembers
to fetch 'Paddy's gossun' (by car, if you please!)
while there's still any light in the sky.

But now I fast-forward another five decades
to join the long line in Battery Park
for the ferry to bring us to Ellis Island,
the spot where you landed, so near yet so far.

And I'm counting the steps to the processing hall
under scrutiny from ghostly medical men
on the lookout for wheezing, the telltale sweats
that warrant the button hook under the eyelid.
I'm guessing you skipped this, already too ill,
being stretchered ashore to Contagious Diseases,
a fevered lone adult among all the children
who would likely recover, as you would not,
the ward decorated with this loveless warning:
'DO NOT, REPEAT NOT, KISS A PATIENT!'

And I'm swapping the horse-drawn hearse for the subway
to St Raymond's Cemetery up in The Bronx,
your sisters, chief mourners, with sundry cousins,
some funeral parlour or overnight chapel
all faded away in the mists of their pain.
But your grave is still willing to welcome the visit
urged on me by elderly aunts who insist
there's room for one more only all of their own
are scattered, a damn shame it's going to waste:
And we might share a joke about this 'real estate'
that was 'bijoux', boasting of 'very quiet neighbours'
and regret that we're helpless to act in the matter
for in death, as in life, it's bureaucracy rules
and God alone knows where's the deeds.

So, farewell to Vincent 'Mad Dog' Coll and 'Lady'
I'm whisking you back to the Kingdom of Breffni
Though there's not a soul left on this side of the mountain
and your own home that boasted an extra half-storey,
a ceili-house favoured the length of the parish,
has fallen in round us, a shelter for stock.
If we stand at the tree where your brother, my father,
encountered what surely had been the banshee,
the eye will be drawn to what will outlast us
the massive sheep-pen, – there! – above on the hill
that you and your siblings built stone upon stone

and I conjure them all out of rhyme's reverie:
Oweny and Maimy and Helen and Pee
And Tommy and Paddy and Lucy and Bee.

Grey stone, grey water
Stony grey soil of Monaghan
A hand-wringing small grey squirrel
Emerges, soaking with grey dew
– your first grey hairs:
A young eel, greasy grey
The grey wing upon every tide
Where mouse-grey waters are flowing,
The surface of a slate-grey lake
Leaving an ash-grey sky

Grey Belfast dawn illuminated me
The gray waters of The Moyle
A grey crow from an old estate
Shuddering up the grey lough
Grey-blue above Belfast
The grey past is dead
Battleship-grey-faced kids
Forsake the grey skies for the blue;
When you are old and grey
The mind stays grey, obtuse, inert

We answer to no grey South
Among grey eighteenth-century houses
Or on the pavements grey
Gray flashing windows of a nineteenth century boutique
And the gray horizon putting up the shutters
Three grey sisters share an eye
Grey is the colour of the coin they give
While a window goes slowly grey;
There is grey in your hair
And the world and the day are grey and that is all

A grey eye will look back
Back into the grey flesh of Donegal

Washed on that coast by the grey sea
Of the Grey of Macha, Cuchulain's horse
Grey hair blinds her eyes
Grey-black embers colder than any cold
And their grey crust grew on me
A greyness like a dye darkening the page
Has come to its zenith of grey spite
In that grey veined dark

The painter lost his sense of all but grey
One high star chilling in a grey, bleak sky
A stand of greyish tapering ash
The branches were twisted and nude, grey
Strategic grey birds rose up from the roots
In the grey point of the briar;
Still bell in hand, eyeing grey swans
And the grave grey of the sea
Grey ash on a poised cigarette
And your face grown cold and grey.

On Not Winning The Patrick Kavanagh Award for the Umpteenth Time

I mailed my poems to Monaghan,
brown paper wrapped, tied up with cord,
ten pounds enclosed to help me win
The Patrick Kavanagh Award

The poems were rural, the meal bin,
the turf stack and the new-mown sward,
in form and rhyme designed to win
The Patrick Kavanagh Award

They tarried here and there with Sin
and held a note of bleak discord.
I hungered for the day I'd win
The Patrick Kavanagh Award

They showed the woman deep within:
my muse, my oracle, my Gord-
ian Knot, one snip and I would win
The Patrick Kavanagh Award

My hopes, alas, were paper-thin.
They failed to strike the proper chord
and (feck 'em!) judged unfit to win
The Patrick Kavanagh Award

For Angels dancing on a pin,
The North in peaceable accord
are safer bets than me to win
The Patrick Kavanagh Award

I should have held on to my tin
for, truth to tell, I doubt, O Lord,
if Patrick Kavanagh would win
The Patrick Kavanagh Award!

THOMAS MCGUIRE

Thomas McGuire's poems, literary translations and creative non-fiction have appeared in *North American Review*, *The Southeast Review* and *War, Literature & the Arts* (*WLA*). He recently completed his first poetry collection, *Becoming Magpie*. An Associate Professor at the US Air Force Academy, he also serves as Poetry Editor for *WLA*. He has published scholarship in the fields of war literature and contemporary Irish poetry and translation. Currently, he's finishing a manuscript entitled *Violence and the Work of Translation: Transformational Forces in the Seamus Heaney Archive*. In 2008, he received a Fulbright Fellowship to Ireland, where he lectured and researched intersections of violence and culture.

I'm a bizarre bird with varied voices;
Audubon says my song is *queg* or *maag*,
But I can howl like a hound, bleat like a lamb
Honk like a honker, shriek like a shrike.
At times I mock the ash-grey eagle –
His battle-bird's cry. The vulture's croak
And, so too, the lovely mew of the curlew
Roll trippingly, grippingly off my tongue
As I sit here sauced. Pie completes my name;
Maggot begins it and eats the end.

Who am I?[1]

This poem is a liberal, updated translation of Riddle 24 in the *Book of Exeter*. It is one of the runic riddles. A more literal translation of the poem's final lines reads, 'They name me *Giefu*, likewise *Ac* and *Rad*. *Os* supports me, *Hægl* and *Is*. Now I am called this just as these six staves clearly betoken'. *The runes spell H I G O R A, or magpie.*

With wife and kids away, he cleared a space for dalliance. He scooped a tablespoon full of everything on the counter – mashed potatoes, peas and turnips, kielbasa. He stuffed it all into his gob. This was his little secret, performed in solitude. He chewed, rolled it all up into one ball, then spat it on the plate. *Thud*. Repeating the process, he launched another ball. *Thud*. Nothing like that familiar empty morning sound, the metallic ring of children pouring cereal into breakfast bowls. *Thud*. Sound of substance. He admired the way the orbs looked. Like haggis. *Haggis* – strange word. So foreign and familiar. Three times he said the weird word: *Haggis, haggis, haggis*. Ah, from *l'agace*, of course, he mused. *L'agace*: French, some sort of bird word, he recalled. Repeating the word slowly, he stressed each syllable. Making strange was in his larynx, in his bones. He liked the sensation generated by the word vibrating off his tongue, thrumming under the roof of his mouth. Mouth music. The sound pleased him. He longed now to see the word spelled out. Into his phone, then, he typed *l'agace*. Letter by letter the word materialized. Miraculous: through an intragalatic tap, one could uncover a bird word, dig deep into its fossil record. *L'agace*: perhaps from *hachheiz*, Old French for *minced meat*, which gave way to *l'agace*, French for 'magpie'. Analog of the odds and ends collected by the bird or perhaps a nod to the fowl's appetite for raw flesh. He felt more hunger rumble, gurgle in his gut. He bit and chewed again, but now sans fork. He ate directly by the beak. He chewed, minced the mélange, rolled it up into one ball, then watched it drop and fall upon his plate. *Hachheiz*, he said. Too Germanic. He much preferred saying, hearing the lovely, tender French *l'agace*. How smoothly it lilted off the tongue; he spoke the word again, slowly, lovingly, mouthing each vowel gradient, feeling letter by strange letter, the sweet tension of each syllable's soft explosion within his gob. *L'agace, l'agace, l'agace* is what he said before slipping into a whispered *Magpie, Magpie, Magpie*.

HOLDING STILL BECOMING MAGPIE

*I saw [in photographs] how St Thérèse existed from the life of an
ordinary young lady to that of the nun. So everything was actual and I
went on writing.*
– Gertrude Stein

In Gertrude's landscapes nothing really moves
But things are there like magpies in the air
Over the fields of Avila or Lisieux –

Holding still the birds lie flat upon the sky,
As in Annunciation scenes where the Holy Spirit rests,
Pressed high and level against the heaven.

None of which is possible in actuality. Birds can't hold still
In flight, to hang suspended in a blue and cloudless sky.
Yet Saints do say, *With God everything's possible, all shall be well.*

So's the suggestion in the grainy image train: a girl is first
A longhaired lass, then frame by frame she becomes
A shorn nun, an icon of magpiety in white and black.

What's more bold and beautiful than a shorn, silent nun –
A bird of black & white, holding still, pressed flat
    against the sun?

GERTRUDE STEIN ON A SOUL'S MIRACULOUS MIGRATION TO MAGPIETY

On the Boulevard Raspail
there floats a place on watery air
where they fashion photographs,

pictures that I've always loved.
There they craft image after
image of a young girl dressed

in the costume of ordinary life
and little by little, slowly
in a photographic river-run

she transforms into a nun:
a saint, uncomplicated,
selfless, in black and white,

light and darkness indivisible –
a momento mori of forty still lifes
for friends and family when

the girl is dead, in memoriam.

MAGPIE: FEEDER OFF BATTLEFIELDS

With a heart joyous nor scared by its own rapacity,
Magpie looks about and below a bank of clouds
Bedizening orange and daffodilly skies,
He spies killing fields spread all before him –
A world not changed since the first blood-dimmed tide
Came roiling in, that morning when, somewhere East
Of Eden, Cain conked Abel, the day that wombed
The never-healing wound, a wound still unbound,
Rubbed forever raw and round by brothers killing brothers,
Unworlding wounds of battlegrounds filled by mounds
    On mounds of tombs –

    〰

On abandoned bison-roads that cleave the precious line
Between ripe and rot he roams. In troughs of feed
Which others might find awful and repulsive,
So breeds and multiplies the mystery of this bird,
This fowl so strange, a corvid curious and carnivorous,
Who loves whatever's weird (the worst of dregs and dirges),
Slaughters for a living, feeds and feasts off battlefields,
Butchering songs of life and death, strains ever ancient,
Ever new, *unheimlich* sights and sounds
About what's hidden out of sight, yet somehow beautiful,
Strange things heard and only seen by
Those who know the worth of laying low,
Ears cocked to the ground, bodies bowed reverently
Before pretty birds deceased and munching maggots.

LAVENDER AND WORMWOOD
for Gary Snyder

gods made by human hands are not gods at all
– St Paul to the silversmiths of Ephesus

Wormwood is sacred to Artemis. Narrow leaves glow silver in her moonlight.
– Gary Snyder

When the goddess busked into the ruins
and asked me to dance right there where
Paul had hectored artisans after thinking
too long & hard on Praxitele's busty votive
Artemis, I was whispering to myself,

      What does one say in such a spot
    where a great river's been reduced
    to reeds and lilies in a ditch?
    What does one say to a lover
    whose temple lies in ruins?

So we waltzed through wormwood
while Artemis smelled of lavender, milk
    and venison, a scent which stirred
        not just thoughts of venery
but that no man's hand had made her
and Gary's line that the Greek *artem*
    means *earring*
              as well as *dangle*
------- and I risked whispering in her ear:
    an ear is just an ear without an earring;

her reply was a toothy lobe nip,
and a tongue probe into its parent
which eased our fall into the tall grass
spread along the dark dry bed

of the late *Kücuck Menderez* river,
where we lay beneath the stars.

Then through the silent dark
the huntress sighed: *I know of arts*
in which an ear is more than just an ear
    and with a sudden blow,
straight like an adder,
through the long grass,
she slid and drew me to her under
        that silver slivered moon.

I thought this can't be Artemis –
I've always heard it is the hunt
and not the kill which is the art
    she truly loves … oh god,
I thought, this can't be her.

At which the moon raced behind a cloud,
    and of a sudden she disappeared.

Now I'm left dangling from her memory,
forced to hunt for mortal ears that
I might pierce with this quaint old lay
about our love between the lilies
and the reeds, about our tenderness
above the watercress and moss –
    oh, love among the ruins.

ETHNA MCKIERNAN

Ethna McKiernan has been twice awarded a Minnesota State Arts Board grant in poetry. Her first book was nominated for the Minnesota Book Award and her work has been widely anthologized, including in *The Notre Dame Book of Irish American Poetry, 33 Minnesota Poets* and more. McKiernan holds an MFA from Warren Wilson Program for Writers. Her fourth book, *Swimming With Shadows,* is due from Salmon Poetry in March 2019. McKiernan works in Street Outreach for a non-profit serving the Minneapolis homeless population. In an earlier life, she was CEO of Irish Books and Media, Inc.

St. James Orphan

It was surrounded by enormous high prison-like walls. Entrance was gained through a great doorway, permanently closed. It was in this doorway, a century or so ago, that a little revolving contraption had been inserted into which mothers placed babies for whom they could no longer care. By turning it around, they could send the little child into the awful prospect of almost certain death in the workhouse.
– Noel Browne, *Against the Tide*

Mother

As if we had a choice.
The three-penny upright on the street
who lifts her tired skirts to faceless men
didn't choose, either; no more
than my body planned to spill out
five weak babies, the lump sum
of my husband's blunt hunger.

I've seen their faces
in the shadows of St. James,
those other mothers parting with young flesh.
If looks could kill, this city'd
reek of death.

You were my smallest one,
little runt among the sparrows,
lame last-born girl.
'Suffer the children', Father Conroy says,
but I don't believe it any more.

Child

They wake you arguing.
You've heard the words so many times
by now they seem a lullaby:
too many mouths, the bread's run out,

no coal, one boy, three girls,
again another girl.
The song ends like a warped psalm,
And you sleep.

Your mama whispers that it's just a dream,
dresses you in winter knickers,
the Sunday-best grey dress. Her kisses
heat the pre-dawn cold. You sleepwalk
through the Dublin slums
to walls that block the sky of light,

then she lets go your hand.
One world ends
as you watch your mother's face
closing for the last time
while the small shelf
slowly swings you into darkness.

MY FATHER'S ROLODEX

The blunt black letters
have begun to fade after 14 years.
Flipping the cards on the wheel
I see decades of history swarm
before me, some of the entries
in the old Irish script, some
in his usual clean, dense print.
How I know that certain hand,
the strong stroke of alphabets
connecting continents, New England
east to Ireland, the Midwest after;
how that hand grew trembly
with the years, the lines wavering
into a fine gibberish.

I look down again
and the card-stock pages
turn to miniature leaves flicking
years from past to present
till they arrive at vibrant strength,
my father at his desk grading papers
on Keats and Yeats and Dickinson,
the Dublin phonebook
always on the shelf behind him,
book piles like towers
growing up beside his feet.
Now he's on the phone, smiling,
fingers penning another entry
to the rolodex as he sips his tea
and speaks. And I am watching all
of this from the doorway of the future
where he no longer walks or writes,
the old rolodex on his desk
like a stilled animal. And oh my father,
what I'd give.

OUR ANCESTRAL GHOSTS

The tall shadow from the roof at Sheeaun
forms a dark vee across the lawn lit with stars
behind the house belonging to my brother Fergus.
Calm settles like a sigh upon the town below,
and a low wind forms a scrim
upon the surface of Lough Derg
a half mile beneath the house.

I have come to see the yellow gorse
of County Clare where my grandmother
was born, the rocky landscape past
the Burren that leads straight to the sea,
the fuschia and foxgove-studded hills
she walked before she left for New York.

Look, see how this house holds
a part of her, holds my brother's fiddle music
as it echoes through the kitchen at Sheeaun
each night, reaching back from the future
to her ears while she stands and stares at the sea,
humming to herself a forward tune; see how
we hold our ghosts of history dear.

'Mirror, mirror on the wall'
was how the whole thing started,
my stepmother trembling at the threshold
of middle age, her radiant beauty
just about to fade. Innocent
of the mirror's lure, I wore my black hair
in straight braids, knew each tree
in the forest by its bark, conversed
with thrush and lark as I played.

So you can see that when the prince
plucked the poisonous apple
from between my lips,
I couldn't bear the joy in his eyes.
What lay ahead was someone else's destiny,
tiresome curtseys and the weight of a crown;
a closet full of wasp-waisted dresses
and villagers 'your highnessing' me
right and left, with all the expectations
of a man who'd saved my life
waiting for me in bed at night.

All I'd really wanted was to dwell
in harmony among the dwarves,
playing Scrabble at the breakfast table
with the little men I loved, Doc and Sleepy
waving as they walked out the door
to the mines, Bashful and Dopey
singing a duet while we washed the morning dishes.

But the drama's fizzled into history
long ago – the huntsman who spared my neck,
the trick of combs and apples, the fact
of my survival. God knows why,
but one morning I unbound my braids

and stepped into the palace for the first time.
My hair slid down my shoulders
and I shivered as it settled
on the weight of red brocade below.

How I miss playing house
with that band of doting dwarves,
how I can't explain to Hans
I preferred the apple in my throat
to this queenship I pretend is mine.

THE WAY BACK

And what if I'd gone *this* way
and not that, so many years back?

At the crossroads, two tall glasses,
maybe water, maybe wine.

One stone sings to the other
of its loneliness, and they meet downstream.

Regret's a layered sentiment, shapeshifting
the mountain sideways;

gratitude, contentment, twin flowers
growing upright from bare rocks.

You kissed me, a sear. I remember
now. Tang of pine, forest air.

If the meadow is this high today
and this purple, surely you are there?

DAVID MCLOGHLIN

Among other themes, David McLoghlin's work examines the complications of emigrating to the USA both as a child and an adult, and the experience of surviving clerical sexual abuse. His books are *Waiting for Saint Brendan and Other Poems* and *Santiago Sketches* (Salmon, 2012 and 2017). *Crash Centre*, his third collection, is forthcoming. *Sign Tongue*, his rendering of the work of Chilean poet Enrique Winter, won the 2014 Goodmorning Menagerie Chapbook-in-Translation prize. His work has been broadcast on WNYC's Radiolab and published widely. He has lived in New York City since 2010, where he works in the not-for-profit sphere.

PORN KING

Afternoon to evening behind a daytime curtain
things go fuzzy and white, hopscotching inside the
    honeycomb:
TV with spag bol (two-and-a-half portions), Kenco instant;
two beers, three, then carpet-burn: the mood bath so warm
and soft it verges on fibreglass, like being wrapped in
    cotton wool.
A finger from a saint's hand – or some other wanker –
a relic from the days of Dial-Up. 1995 and 1996,
spent disassociating.

    *

It takes so long to load I mutter 'bollox', and go to make tea
instead. In my absence, a woman's head smiles
waiting for her body to arrive. The modem hisses, *Krrs. Krrsss*:
the sound of something coming down the line. It recalls
the documentary's solemn intoning, an imagined 'end via
    black hole'
where I elongate like taffy in the event horizon,
and then am obliterated, pixel by pixel.

    *

Before we knew about webmail, and put our trust in hosts
out on the ether, my parents paid for ann-, brian-, ruth-,
david-, rebecca- and marc-, all snug @islandhouse.iol.ie.
When email was domain-specific, visiting my parents, itchy
for something half decent, I used Dad's email address
to subscribe. Back in Dublin, I got the call: 'David, I got
this strange email from' – then he italicized – '*XXX*.com'.
Pause. 'Your mother *feels* pornography is degrading
    to women'.
My head bowed, nodding, a dripping tap. After that
my sister's boyfriend called me *The Porn King*.

In boarding school, we were 15 when Ricky Roche liberated
a mag, *Oui*, out of his father's arsenal. Ten of us crowded round,
a compound eye intent on the couple, frozen
fucking on the bonnet of a yellow Ferrari. She: amazing,
straw-blonde; he, only relevant in equipment terms. Incredible
positioning and nothing for the imagination. One by one
we crept back to tear pieces for wank fodder,
until all that was left was ads for vibrators and bad prose.

*

Two years later, me and Fr. Terence sit in the monastery
guest kitchen, just beyond the lintel that marks the enclosure.
The distance between sacred and secular
is Zeno of Elea slicing space, like meat you can see through,
or Occam's razor. Terry's legs are crossed under his black robe:
Friar Tuck in Birkenstocks and polyester socks. He says, 'David,
I've something to show you'. And out from a manila folder,
from a sheaf of papers with *Nihil Obstat* all over them,
he passes me a magazine. '*Well*,
we've been talking about your sexuality, so I thought
this might help. What do you think? Do you like that?'

My hands are turning pages of naked men. 'I don't know',
    I say.
He's my best friend. I have to please him. Why am I afraid?
Bulbs explode behind my eyes: like paparazzi, or
    pornographers
crowding round, jostling for a piece of me. I go
into another room, multiverse and string theory, and
    navigate away
on my maiden voyage, solar wind. An alarm is ringing,
but the tongue's been taken from the bell.

*

Years later – who tracks the years lost to it? – at a party
I gather some friends, go up the spiral stairs to my father's
        study,
input a password on a site where I have membership.
        Compulsion is
not even thinking to ask *why?* Everyone acts naturally.
Now I imagine the happy couples, pillow talking:
'Why do you think he showed us hardcore pornography?'

                *

Once or twice during pillow fuckery, it happened:
I am close to the laptop screen, so intent that my optic
        nerve
and eye are outside my body, like a schematic
from Leaving Certificate Biology: something lopped off
but still connected. The actress – acted upon –
is looking into the camera. Suddenly she meets my eye.
Help me.

THE DRYING ROOM

From the Senior showers it was less than five minutes
to the monastery – where I went after supper
the day Fr. Terence said: 'See you over in Reception
at eight, then. Have a shower, and make sure
that you're very clean'.
I was warm wax for his signet ring,
his appraising smile during our first kiss,
around the time I gave up rugby.

After training in rain or sleet, grit glittered in mud
and your own blood was in it.
Shorts forgotten a day in the changing room
were lost in a ferment, like a slurry pit.

In the Drying Room, gear got crunchy, coiling the wall pipes.
Thinking aloud, like shoppers, Seniors said: 'I need …
socks'. And took a younger boy's. I almost liked it:
getting into dry, utterly dirty gear, the natural filth.
As if your jersey had shingles: mud plaques
nervous-brittle, toasty against your back
standing in the Tenebrae of humming pipes.

On match days, the air stung with *Deep Heat*.
We faced each other, sitting, thoughtful, vaselining
then taping down our ears. We taped our fingers,
black tape among the white, hands gritted for purchase,
our wrists cooled to the hilt in powdered bone.
Our gum shields were in,
we ourselves were weaponised,
had put on bronze greaves. Our gear was laundered,
our faces pale with adrenaline.

Sean Donovan, the American prop, genuflected
for a private *Our Father*, then stood, slapping backs.
Shouting started, like an orchestra tuning towards a note.

Then we circled. Clasp. Touch.
– And go. The run down to the pitches from the castle
was a flying column. I could hear the crowd,
metal studs on loose tar macadam,
the coaches' fat voices, winded
 – 'like a pack of wolves, Glen!' –
The subs were running with us,
loyalty sparking from the ground.
12-year-old boys shouted our names,
Mothers stood as we sprinted past, their Hoplites.

Sometimes I have wanted to go back, in order to remain
standing in my stained uniform among the mayhem
of school colours, the way I stood before a match
as if I was being cinched into a breastplate
by my grave squire, as if my own battle waited,
a quarter-inch of petrified mud-flakes under our boots
in the far corner of the Drying Room,
where I have wanted to stay
in the radius of Sean's prayer.

– Terry was saying, 'Among the Athenians, inspiration was
an older man with a younger man: inspiring him – literally
inspiring. So, make sure that you're very clean'. He kept on
repeating 'clean' – jocular, lulling. Only now
– I can hear the italics. I was by myself
under the showerheads. I washed my hair,
and lathered my privates, twice.
I didn't understand he had meant my anus.

I oiled my ponytail, and over that unction
was my favourite skull cap.
My Doc Marten eight-holes were on
and my Crombie swung open
like a First World War greatcoat. I went down
the flagstones, past Matron's circular room
at the tower's base, where our teachers took port

by the fire, nightly, I went down
the steep wooden stair to exit
under the arch that read *Pax*.

No one told me to go the lesser-used way, but I did.
I felt something – but so far off, it was years away
in the mind's snowfields, in the core samples.
As my hand felt along the moss on the monastery wall,
the jerseys wrapping the pipes
ghosted for arms, holding on.

CENTRAL PARK, NOCTURNE
The living iguanas will come to bite the men who don't dream
'City Without Sleep (Nocturne of the Brooklyn Bridge)'
– Federico García Lorca.

Black trees – a little snow. People pause, deferring
to their expensive dogs: maybe find a moment like
    breviary.
From the reservoir, in failing light the buildings park-side
are Angkor-Wat accretion, or a mud city in Mali.
'Gateway of the oasis'. City of the wolf and the iguana.
My childhood and future seem to have departed
to go jaunting down empty paths under lamplight
– electricity mimicking gas light – in a park in Europe:
the Retiro's sandy paths, maybe even Phoenix Park.
Leaf preserved in grey ice. White ambergris.
Yellow hexagonals corona, come on high up,
hive-like, extending, silent. Night's calm black,
undersurfacing.

RAY MCMANUS

Ray McManus is the author of three books of poetry: *Punch.* (Hub City Press, 2014), *Red Dirt Jesus* (Marick Press, 2011) and *Driving through the Country before You Are Born* (USC Press, 2007) and co-editor of the anthology *Found Anew* (USC Press, 2015). McManus is a Professor of English at the University of South Carolina Sumter, where he directs the SC Center for Oral Narrative. He also serves as Writer in Residence at the Columbia Museum of Art and is Chair of the Board of Governors for the South Carolina Academy of Authors.

DIEHARDS

I'm dying.
My wife is dying.
Our kids are dying.
Their pets are dying.

The neighbors are dying.
The tree out back is dying,
and the field behind it
is dying again.

The road is not dying,
but everything on it is:
every bone cycle,
every skin machine.

My wife pats the backseat,
wakes the kids and says look.
Their eyes are wide open
in the rearview mirror.

Manifest Destiny

For the pump of it, the drop, the brake, the tongue,
the anus, the nipple pointed against the sunlight
under the visor – I'll be the first to admit it.
I'll do anything. For a new sun to shimmer
before it explodes into a million suns.
For all that's left of you and me to cool the engine.
For the ride on the two-lane past the swamp,
past the blockhouses and garages where boys break
radios to fan belt overtures before they die.
For the fact that I know I won't miss them
                                        and never did.

For the damp of it. For the turns we'll take
where imaginations race shadows, and I'll think
what I could do if I could be you if you just let me
and you let me. For the grind it takes to be an engine.
For the timing it takes to turn everything over,
to stay tuned, to stay hard, to stay tuned again –
this isn't magic. This isn't a mystery either –
compression, fire, the death that comes
from the exhaust of it, from the boredom of it.

In town, people look the same, wear the same,
speak in same to same. It's all the same:
no machines to wrestle, no boys waiting
to die in open bays. Just windows stuffed
with paper, vinyl covering the brick.
In town, people keep their hands to themselves,
train their eyes to see both ways before crossing –
bodies shaped to live cautious and deliberate –
but they never look.

                    This can't be our country.

For the love of it, the pledge of it,
the word for it,

                  this cannot be our country.

For the destination we'll reach in union.
For ratification. For surges
between the scar and the shoulder.
For a nation we should've forgotten in the first place.
For the fastest route from savagery to decadence.
For my palm and your palm at the edge of the swamp
For what we'll call *here*.
For what we'll call *now*.
Here, where we can't trick out the word.
Now, where there is no word.
Just you and me by our divine right,
surveying the space between us,
taking it, and calling it ours.

CAVEMAN BIAS

My neighbor is all tongue
and twisted lip.
All plastic hip and napalm.
All belt and broken motor.
A gift, some might say,
from a heartless god.

And at the hottest part of the day
when most of us have taken
to quieter comforts, he stands
in his yard pistol tight
and ready to take out snakes.

My neighbor was born a Cadillac,
not a Caprice Classic not a Cutlass Supreme.
An ornament unhooded.
All back surgery and wrecking ball.
All bumper bent around a frame.

His face searches for the shadow
from his visor. He races backwards
as if it's better than standing still,
and his Saturday evenings are wrecked
by kids not yet bound
by imaginary lines.

My neighbor will blame me
for poor slope and lack of backfill,
how rocks are not brick,
how the voices of my children crash
through his window.
But my neighbor doesn't talk
like a parent, doesn't work the angles
the way we do when we're scared.

My neighbor is all Rambo and Vronsky.
All blood in the throat.
All hard bark before it falls to the ground.
And snakes, like kids mostly, are harmless,
like neighbors when left alone.

Some say snakes are just
looking for a nest that's not like home,
a place to rest if swollen after a meal.
Sometimes they get stuck there.
Everything is capable of being.
Everything is capable of being unwanted.

My neighbor has been here
longer than anyone.
Longer than a neighborhood
or a heartless god.
Longer than a bullet.

My neighbor is the wind that dies on a face.

My neighbor says hello when he sees a snake
stretched next to the tree line,
and kills it anyway.

My neighbor is all fist
for the right-handed,
all tumor and revolt.
All pit and strike.

He'll be here longer than anyone.
Just ask the snake.

HOW TO FORGET A NATION

My first mistake: the row of rocks
used to mark the border.

My second mistake
was showing you.

Rocks, I explained, leave a mark.
That too was a mistake.

Tonight, I'll move them back
where I found them.

In all honesty,
I don't know where they go.

I say this facing the dark
because it's easier to lie that way

because it's easier to come from nothing
if I just keep going nowhere.

I know nothing about rocks or borders
beyond what I've been told.

I don't know where they come from,
why they're just sitting here waiting

for someone like me to pick one up
and rub the flat side, the messy side.

I don't even know which side is which.
I never thought to ask.

UNDERTOW

Stand on a beach
on the east coast,
and stare at the ocean
while the sun sets,
look for a nation
that doesn't know you.
You will see God.

Look to the ocean,
not the sun.
The ocean gives up
its scattered heart
and takes it back.

The ocean whispers
look behind you,
it's all behind you.

The ocean, like the sun,
does not know you,
does not owe you
a goddamned thing.
You – a goddamned thing.

Go to it.
Feel it.
Feel all of it.
The sun on your back.
The tide on your face.
And while you breathe, hope
the ocean swallows you whole.

JOHN MENAGHAN

A prize-winning poet and playwright, John Menaghan has published four books with Salmon Poetry: *All the Money in the World* (1999), *She Alone* (2006), *What Vanishes* (2009) and *Here and Gone* (2014). A fifth book, composed entirely of jazz-related poems, is forthcoming. His poems have appeared in *Ambit*, *The Hopkins Review*, *Brilliant Corners*, *Poetry Ireland Review*, *Atlanta Review*, *American Arts Quarterly* and other places. He has been nominated for a Pushcart Prize in four of the last six years, several of his short plays have received performances, and one – *A Rumor of Rain* – appeared in *The Hollow & Other Plays* (2008).

BLESSING

A man and woman somewhere in their 30s,
drifting through the dirty streets of Dublin
in a highly altered condition, dirty as well,
hair and clothes in disarray, with an air
of urgently searching for something they
half expect never to find and who wouldn't
be able to say what it is they're seeking if
you asked and may not even know they are.

Yet as they pass the open door of a church,
the woman takes a quick look in, then
blesses herself, executing a rapid-fire
sign of the cross while pausing so briefly
imperceptibly the man seems not even aware
of her attention or forward motion having
been ever so fleetingly arrested let alone
her gesture, bent as he is on making good
time on his arduous journey to perdition.

SWEETNESS
Ben Webster

I think if you try all the different
styles in vogue you con yourself.
Me, I just stick by my guns. Don't
want to play from another man's bag.

I'm out to stir your heart and soul with
every phrase, embrace each note, my throat
producing airy breaths of sound like voices
whispering sighs between the sheets.

I like to play things people understand,
or maybe just tunes they can recognize.
I play for the people as much as for
Myself – because I do still like to play.

When I die, ship my old carcass to K.C.
and bury me deep in its dark brown loam.
But keep Ol' Betsy for me, only don't
let anyone else play her – never again.

They'll say I drank too much. Too true.
Made me a brute sometimes. True too.
But there was plenty of sweetness inside.

And when it oozed through my tenor
like a caress, it could really take hold of you.
Make you feel finer than anyone you knew.

BIRD DIES
Charlie Parker

What does it really mean to be on the wing?
How many notes can I put in the same tune?
What kinds of dreams are the best ones for me to have?
What will the world make of me when I'm dead and gone?

Don't say: I don't know the answers. Nobody does.
Don't fret if waking up is beyond you somehow.
Follow the path even if it goes nowhere fast.
Things could be worse, man. You'll never grow old.

Play the tune quick as you can, I always felt.
Seems like there's plenty of time? Not as much as you think.
What's time, anyhow? Something you keep, then discard.
Everyone's got one – a last night on this earth.

Bird lives. Bird dies. Bird flies away.
I can't help myself. And if I can't nobody can.

JANIS JOPLIN, MY MOTHER & ME

I was sitting at the kitchen table
while my mother hovered
(like Mother Hubbard, I
want to say, but did she,
I don't have a clue, but
my mother did, definitely,
frequently, expertly)
around the sink the fridge
the stove the counter me –
it was a small kitchen –
did I mention I now live alone
in a house twice the size
of the one once housed my
grandmother, my parents and
four children yet sometimes
still seems too small for me –
and for once I guess I'd spun
the dial on the radio and we
were listening – well, I was,
sorta kinda like, who knew
about Mom – to some decent
music instead of boring old John
Gambling who my mother never
got tired of telling us couldn't
compare to his late great father
for gab when suddenly on comes
Janis Joplin rasping away on
'Get It While You Can' and my mother
must have been listening now cause
she said, 'That poor girl', and I
looked up from my breakfast
(must have been a weekend if John
wasn't on) and said: 'What?'
'That poor girl', my mother
said again, even sadder sounding

this time, 'to die so young'.
We listened together a moment
while I tried to think what to say
and then, as Janis sang *Don't you know*
when you're lovin' somebody, babe,
You're takin' a chance on a little sorrow,
Mom chiming in again:
'I never cared for her music, mind you.
Still, how sad to die like that. So
all alone. Let that be a lesson
to you now what drugs can do'.
Jesus, I thought to myself, it's
too early in the morning for this
and I'm too old for lessons
from my mother, I mean
I'm in high school for godsakes
not kindergarten so I just
sat there thinking up a
bunch of smartass remarks
to make like 'Well, at least
she lived before she died'
or 'Actually, she wasn't
poor by the time she died,
she was rich' or 'Maybe she
just took the *wrong* drugs'
or 'She was a woman,
Mother, not a girl') but
before I could choose my
mother'd gone off to hover
somewhere else for a bit
so there I was alone when it
came flooding back Janis
on Dick Cavett talking about
how she's headed back to her
high school reunion and cackling
about the reaction she'll get and how
surprised they'll all be to see her

and Cavett says 'Not anymore'
and she puts her hand to her mouth
like a little girl who's let a bad word
slip through her lips and fears
being punished for it but then
says 'Oh, well, what the hell'
and smiles but somehow looks
terribly sad at the same damn time
and dies not very long after while
my mother goes on about her day
and her life and lives another 30
years and dies at the ripe old
age of 89 and though there's no
videotape, no cd to reissue, that scene
my mother likely forgot the moment
she left the kitchen plays over and over
in my brain each time I hear Janis'
saucy, insouciant voice echoing through
my big empty house singing *Who cares,*
baby, cause we may not be here tomorrow
and I think of them both gone now
to who knows where but maybe together
comparing notes and I miss them both
terribly though of course in different
ways till I hear Janis cackling away
at me while my mother, a gentler
soul but one whose life had its share
of blues, hovers just beside her,
looking down on me, and says
with a sigh, 'That poor boy, look
at him, Janis, seared with sorrow
over losing us, while here we are
watching over him together if he
only knew it, but he always did
think he knew it all'. 'Smartass
little bastard', Janis says, that Mona
Lisa smile spreading across her lips

while my mother just shakes her head
and says again, even sadder sounding
this time, 'That poor boy, divorced,
you know, so young, so long ago'.
And Janis silent now for once, at a loss
for words, then my mother again,
'I never cared for his wife, mind you,
Still, how sad to live like that. So
all alone. Let that be a lesson
to you now what love can do'.

ANN NEELON

Ann Neelon traces her roots to the historically Boston Irish enclave of Dorchester, where she began her teaching career at Boston College High School. She is currently a Professor of English at Murray State University in western Kentucky. The recipient of the Regents Teaching Award, she directed MSU's low-residency MFA program from 2010 to 2016 and edited *New Madrid* journal from 2006 to 2018. Her collection of poems *Easter Vigil* won both the Anhinga Prize for Poetry and the Returned Peace Corps Volunteer Writers and Readers Award. Previous honors include a Stegner Fellowship and Jones Lectureship, both from Stanford University.

Because it was early spring.

Because someone in Dinand Library had started a rumor.

Because we had gotten sick of staring into the dead zones
of snow in the deep shadows of trees behind
Loyola.

Because nakedness was a uniform. We had to prove we
were capable of wearing one too.

Because it was the dawn of a new era. Men, the last of
them, were getting zipped into body bags and
shipped home from Viet Nam.

Because, standing naked on the quad, we were so nervous
about being accused of being perverts that we were
fixating on each other's *upper* upper bodies.

Because we were shivering. If we didn't start running,
we'd die of hypothermia.

Because we didn't know whether to say 'streaked' or
'struck'.

Because someone said *it's now or never*.

Because my father, an alumnus, had told me you had to
get up pretty early in the morning to fool the
Jesuits.

Because, once in a while in the old days, young men had
succeeded in doing so.

Because, if his friend had overslept, a young man would
step up at mandatory Mass to be counted twice.
Coats and ties were like uniforms. It was hard for
the old priests, especially, to tell the young men
apart.

Because a lot of us felt as if the dead boys had stepped in
for us or for our brothers.

Because it was like the men in our class had overslept
history by a few short minutes.

Because it started to rain.

Because it didn't start to rain.

Because the sound of the rain was really the sound of our feet pounding up the hill.

Because everyone who wasn't streaking had gathered at the top of the hill on Easy Street.

Because when they all started clapping, the sound of the rain got louder and louder.

Because nakedness *wasn't* dead bodies.

Because nakedness was the living body.

Because, among the streakers, it was almost impossible to tell who was who, except by their shoes.

Because someone spotted a pair of red sneakers and started chanting, *Johnny O, Johnny O.*

Because you gotta love Johnny O.

Because, on his summer roofing job, he had refused, out of laziness, to climb down from the roof to take a piss.

Because he had pissed instead into what he thought was an empty bucket.

Because it wasn't an empty bucket. It was a bucket slick with the invisible residue of roofing compound.

Because pissing into it was enough to start a blazing fire.

Because old men had come scrambling and swearing from all over the roof to put the fire out.

Because they had abused Johnny O for his stupidity for the rest of the summer.

Because an apocalypse was averted.

Because it wasn't just Johnny O. We were all determined to do enough dumb things to make up for all the dumb things the dead boys couldn't do.

Because we were afraid we were cowards.

Because she was still running toward us on fire, the girl the napalm hit.

Because it was our fault she was burning.

Because, the day after the streak, most of the old Jesuits
      took a pretty dim view of it.
Because Father Bill Schmidt, or Bull Schmidt, as we called
      him, *didn't.*
Because we cherished the linguistic proximity of 'Father
      Bull Schmidt' to 'Father Bull Shit'. Father Bull Shit?
      Bull shit! He was a saint.
Because, in his Sunday sermon, Father Bull Schmidt said
      nakedness was joy.
Because, instead of chastising us, he translated the Latin
      inscription on the front of the chapel:
I will go unto the altar of God, the God who brings joy to my youth.

Because we exalted in our youth.
Because the future was streaking toward us.

His name is Aylan Kurdi.
At first when I see the photo of him lying on the beach
        near the Turkish resort of Bodrum, I think he is
        sleeping, but he is not.
He is identified as a three-year-old Syrian boy.

The day was so hot that the ocean in front of us shimmered
        like a mirage.
A mirage of what?
Eternity?
Suddenly, a strange giddiness possessed my
        three-year-old son.
He descended on me in my beach chair, swooped down on
        my shoulder, stuck out his tongue
and began furiously licking the patch of salt that had
        dried there from an earlier swim.
Stop, I said, *stop. What do you think I am, a salt lick?*

It is the summer of refugees.
They keep coming and coming to Greece – and not just
        from Syria, but from Afghanistan, Pakistan, Sudan,
        Somalia and other countries.
They come in unseaworthy vessels.
It is impossible to feed them all.
It is impossible to house them all.
It is impossible to count the grains of sand on the beach.
Go ahead! Start counting! It would take an eternity to
        make a dent.

All morning, my sons had been hightailing it out to their
        knees in the ocean, filling their pails,
then lumbering back, spilling their precious contents
        along the way.

It would take an eternity, they were on the brink of
        admitting, to fill up the moat around their sand
        castle.
This is because the salt water was draining out as fast
        as they could pour it in.

What looks like boredom in Aylan's father's eyes is grief.
I hope my son's body will serve as an ultimatum to the world,
he says through a translator on every news channel.
He believes his love has proven an unseaworthy vessel.

My five-year-old-son, who had just started whipping a
        dead horseshoe crab around his head
a little further down the beach, came charging back. Then I
        had two small boys
slobbering my sunburned skin at once, laughing
        hysterically despite bumping heads.
Stop, I said. *Stop, stop.*
But they wouldn't stop.

The bodies of Aylan's mother and five-year-old brother
        wash up a few hours later further down the beach
        near Bodrum.

She was the salt of the earth, the salt of the earth.
That's what my mother's friends said to me about my
        mother after waiting in line at the funeral home.

Stop, I said, *stop. What do you think I am, a salt lick?*
Anyway, it was time for lunch.
My sons washed their feet in the bucket on my mother's
        back porch so that they didn't track the sand in.
My mother called them drunken sailors because they
        couldn't stop bumping into everything.
They were so tired they fell asleep on the carpet before I
        could finish making their sandwiches.

I stood in the sunroom for a minute watching their small
       chests rise and fall.
It was like I was floating again in a small boat with my
       father during a flood tide. The ocean and the
       marsh were brimming over.

My father is long dead.
No father's love is an unseaworthy vessel.

When I was a girl and we moved from the city to Green
       Harbor for the summer, I could never sleep. I
       would sneak out of my bedroom, and go lean
       against the seawall.
I could block out horns beeping, brakes squealing.
The ocean was a different story.
I loved listening to its thumping, ta-dum, ta-dum, ta-dum.

It is not Aylan's heart, but the ocean's, beating.

TO THE WOMAN WHO WAS PUSHING A BABY CARRIAGE
DOWN MY STREET AT 5:05 P.M. ON 9/11, RIGHT WHILE
THE INTERVIEWEE I WAS LISTENING TO ON TV WAS
SAYING, *ONE MINUTE I WAS WATCHING A WOMAN PUSH
A BABY CARRIAGE DOWN THE STREET – THE NEXT MINUTE
THE SECOND TOWER COLLAPSED AND SHE DISAPPEARED*

I closed my eyes.
I opened them again.
You were really there.
Thank you for stopping for a second
right outside my living room window
to smooth your newborn's blanket.
His face was like a seed
in the pod of his little suit.

I could have drunk you in wildly, profligately,
guzzling and guzzling, but then I would have burst
from drinking like a heart from love.
I stood very still.
I drank you in slowly, one sip
at a time until you reached
the other end of my street.

Thomas O'Grady

Thomas O'Grady was born and grew up on Prince Edward Island. He is Professor of English and a member of the Creative Writing faculty at the University of Massachusetts Boston, where he has been Director of Irish Studies since 1984. He is the author of two books of poems published by McGill-Queen's University Press: *What Really Matters* (2000) and *Delivering the News* (2019). He divides his time between and among PEI, Milton, MA, and Adamsville, RI and shares domestic life with his wife, three daughters who come and go, and two young cats.

DARK HORSES

Steady to the end,
the limits of his life
defined by fences, hedges,

headlands in a field,
he chose a day of rest
as if he knew the work

could wait, then sought
final comfort circling
square familiar corners,

sniffing for his brother
dark horse death. We
should pray for such grace,

that bred-in-the-bone
knowing what we're called to,
early on: plowing, poeming,

harvesting the sea. Would
that bareback rider raking
Irish moss at Skinner's Pond

agree? In my dream he clutches
madly at a white-flecked mane.
I wake when the anvil ocean bed

leaps up to meet the surging
sledge of beast and tide.

THANKSGIVING

Summers we'd give thanks to be city born
and bred when, come mid-August, our country
cousins trudged two weeks ahead to the stern
task of learning, the clean-cut drudgery
of school. Of course, in October we'd curse
the luck that gave them a fortnight repeal
of break-knuckle rules – though what could be worse
than digging potatoes in muck-caked fields?
Who, in their right minds, would envy that chore,
and pray – in late November, a thousand
miles and many years away – to restore
themselves by the grace of clay-coated hands?
Elbow-deep in a sack of unscrubbed spuds,
we swear never to wash off that red mud.

REDEMPTION

To think that all that time we blamed the spite
of our neighbors – a rabid, demented
pack of God-forsaken, fiend-tormented
curs (though more bark behind our backs than bite) –
on that dismembered Christ, *sans* crucifix,
I unearthed in the garden our first month there,
piercing its heart with the rake's cruel spear:
one of my weekend centurion's tricks.

Jesus wept! If only we had known how
jackals sense calamity in the air –
hovering pestilence, flood, famine, drought:
our fault to have overlooked that horseshoe
hanging wrongside up I found our seventh year.
We left before our luck had all run out.

ALCHEMY

Just our luck. Morning
unloads rain in buckets,
leaden grey. We watch

the sky and wait. We muck
about and pace and place
the day on hold. By noon

we write it off and sigh.
Hours pass. We scoff
at forecasts painted blue.

O ye of little faith! A bold
crow barks a brazen note
of hope behind the barns.

The clouds begin to yield
and lift, pale rays leak through.
Then evening sun erupts.

We walk the lane. Life brightens.
Flooding light weaves braided gold
from a field of sodden grain.

SEEING RED

Blizzard-bound, snowed
under, walled-in ... swallowed
by a whirling world

of white, a mapless maze
of shifting waist-deep drifts,
he wades and wallows.

His hedgerows bent –
though not like ours,
beneath the weight of war

and sorrow ... once more
the winter of our discontent –
he looks ahead as if

to greener pastures.
Hapless cattle lowing
to be fed, he holds his course,

led – as we are too –
by the heartening blaze
of red that frames the doors,

the eaves, the corner trim
of every outlying
Island barn and shed.

AT MCNELLO'S

Hard men. Punters. A thirst for the ponies.
I nursed my pint in the shadows and watched

their equine faces rise then fall as they watched
the Newmarket card play out, race by race,

and, true to form, maligned an afternoon
misspent on a slate of boldly misplaced

wagers: It's My Time, Slip Sliding Away,
Sovereign Debt ... top tips turned to also-rans.

•

Hope. The longshot we ride blinkered every day.
Just ask that loveblind lad behind the bar.

Run ragged, pillar to post, he liked his odds
phoning bets to the bookie's coy daughter.

'A good-looking voice'. He rang up again.
'Tell us her name, boys'. She had him haltered.

Smoke Signals

We shoulder what we can.
The morning sky's red clouds
a warning – *each day aim true* –

I sat astride my two-wheeled steed
and plucked with my mind
the high-strung bow of love.

I knew the trail led home.
What message would I code
that you could read ...

and how deliver? My hands
in the grip of braking, steering ...
I slung across my back

three long-stemmed roses, cellophane-
wrapped. My heart was aquiver.

ELIZABETH ONESS

Elizabeth Oness is a poet and fiction writer who lives on a biodynamic farm in Southeast Minnesota. Her books include: *Articles of Faith, Departures, Twelve Rivers of the Body, Fallibility,* and *Leaving Milan.* Elizabeth directs marketing and development for Sutton Hoo Press, a literary fine press, and is a Professor of English at Winona State University.

DUAL CITIZENSHIP

Out, amidst the corn-heaved fields,
mud and rocks, pine trees and ponies,
past the barn, he is the first kid
on the bus. On a February morning,

even yellow is dark, and he mounts
the phantom vehicle, lights flashing
from the darkened coach. In spite of
its lumbering indirections, he claims

he likes the ride, which means
he likes leaving home without my voice
calling to remind him
of some later plan or forgotten task.

At the road's end, the bus turns.
The war is turning too –
the soldiers coming home,
the stories seeping out.

One soldier tried to rescue a friend
whose brains slipped out
the back of his head.
Brains are heavy, the soldier said.

My son is a citizen of a country
he's never seen. All he knows
are a few bright words: *Dia dhuit.*
Dia's Muire dhuit.

'God go with you'.
'God and the Virgin Mary go with you',
A cynic might say it's competitive
piety, the mother topping off,

but a mother's preparations
are everything and nothing.
Eventually we're all forced
to let go of what we love.

Is This What Poets Do?
for Jody Bolz

Poets try to say that silence tastes
like nickels on the tongue, that winter's

solemn palette is redeemed
by prismed branches in the morning sky.

Poets search for images when they want
to say is *Why did you betray me?*

When did you stop loving me? Flowers taste
like velvet paper, and the raucous picnic

of crows on the ridge hold twigs in their craws
like dark cigarettes. Poets try not

to say the obvious, but language tends
to run downhill and settle in the shallows.

You turn your head and can't erase
what you wish you'd never seen. The body

keeps its memories and it's sorrowing work
to undo what our flesh absorbs.

Today, doing chores, my mind turns over
homophones, my son's vocabulary word.

All we cannot alter becomes a kind of altar,
a place we revisit against our will

because we need the sacred
when we're scared or scarred or both.

LEVERAGE

Five layers of floorboards, each layer a leftover
    from some misbegotten project, each layer nailed
to rotted wood or crumbling particle board
    or burned wood from where a stove once stood.

Forget the examination of arbitrary relationships –
    the gap between signified and signifier –
the cat's paw is sleek black, surly metal, a faceted knob
    with a toe-shaped notch for catching a nail.

I place it over nail heads embedded in the floor,
    hammer the paw to bend the nail head
from its neck. The beetle-backed bar lifts the nail
    to slide the hammer's back into place, and I lean

on the hammer's handle, raise the nail through
    rotted boards, letting leverage do the work.
There's still no electricity in our gutted house, no radio,
    no distraction from old resentments.

Time swells with monotony and effort until my husband
    comes in to move things along. We keep
going forward because there's no going back.
    After months of labor, his knees beneath his jeans

are scraped clean of hair. He reaches for a plank I cannot move,
    his neck muscles widening, and slowly
raises the board. The right tools make the impossible
    possible, but still I envy strength.

TUCK POINTING

Like self-assessment, it becomes necessary with age.
        Between the ochre stones the water-seeped
    cement is mold-dark, crumbling, furring
            rivulet roads where a false window
            led water down the wall.

The old mortar must be chiseled out, swept away,
        fresh mortar tucked in place.
    The halogen light is too bright to face.
            I stab at soft cement, testing what endures
            and what gives way.

Mixing mortar, masked like a movie monster,
        I scoop the bulbous liquid
into a clown-sized pastry bag, squeeze against
        resistance, plug the ledges
        between stones.

Earth presses stone, mortar takes in water. Even limestone
        can't resist earth's seeping,
even granite can't resist the accumulation of tears.
        The mind takes up its reflexive work,
        burrowing into hurt.

An architect once told me, *Anything made by man
        can be fixed by man.*
Mineral veins crumble under probing,
        brittle mortar bleeds to sand
        on the tamped damp floor.

POEM FOR THALIA

The aging broodmares bloom in the meadow
     and lift their noses to the north.

They are a counter-balance to cataracts,
     oxygen tanks, and surgery.

You study the back of the flea-bitten grey,
     her flesh scarred by hooves.

The price of begetting is rippage and scars,
     but after the long winter

her dark teats are waxing and bags
     are growing full.

Cornflower, wild carrot, swallows dipping
     through the barn,

Sunlight on the porch step, the kicked-off Crocs,
     the faded fence.

The mare lies in the pasture, then tries to rise,
     front legs a bridge,

hocks and fetlocks unfolding. She grunts the way
     a tired person pushes from a chair.

Come June, the foal's hooves will be cauled
     by fleshy curls, worn

as they tamp the stones and turf
     of this radiant, dispassionate earth.

It starts with the scent of baking bread on a city wind,
   or a faded ball cap
on the wrong-colored head of hair, or the sound
   of a child's voice
you realize could not be yours. It starts with the memory
of what you looked like before you got sick, rocks forward
with your daughter's caution: *He looks like a pregnant*
   Chinese skeleton.

It starts with the sound of my mother-in-law's voice on the
   phone, telling me what
she made Bill for dinner, and I hear what she does not say
as he waits, in his chair, to be moved to his room. It rounds
   the bend
of memory: my son walking the hillside, the line of his jaw
   no longer a child's.
It starts with the grit of yeast on the counter, the woody
   scent of Asian beetles,
of sun damp earth, of Chinese herbs, of stale beer floating
   from a rotted door.
The track opens onto the unexpected familiar – the spicy
bite of radish, cold scarlet on the tongue, the strains of a
Cars song, which to me means the Eighties, and to my son
is a cool new set of power chords.

We say, in mid-sentence, *I lost my train of thought*, which
   means we lost where
we were going because we forgot where we started, a
   synaptic hiccup,
that train of thought that rushes past the rundown part of town,
the neighborhoods where we once lived, the laundry
   rippling in the evening air,
the dark and blocky ties of our minds, the summoning
   voices hoarse or stilled,
that train of thought whose engine is loss.

DONNA POTTS

Donna L. Potts is professor and chair of English at Washington State University. She is the author of two books in Irish Studies – *Contemporary Irish Poetry and the Pastoral Tradition* and *Irish Literature and Environmentalism: The Wearing of the Deep Green* – as well as a book of poetry inspired in part by Ireland, and published by Salmon Poetry, *Waking Dreams*. She had a Fulbright Senior Lecturing Award at the National University of Ireland in Galway from 1997–98, and has returned there as often as possible ever since.

Villanelle for Johnny Ward

All the best things in life are free –
the man at a Galway shop told her –
but first you have to learn to see.

Swans thundering on strong wings
down the canal under a rich slice of sky –
all the best things in life are free.

A speckled blue bird's egg, chicory flowers,
a rabbit pausing to rest – are worth the view,
but first you have to learn to see.

An old woman gardening looks up and chirps,
'hello pretty girl' as I speed by on a bike:
All the best things in life are free.

A perch in a fork of a weeping willow,
Shade by a river, can hold you all day,
But first you have to learn to see.

Walking in grass with bare feet,
hot air balloons rising in rainbows –
All the best things in life are free.
But first you have to learn to see.

In Donegal

She sits in a pub in Donegal
with an Irishman who once
worked in the states. He sneers
about Yanks, with their prim
little signs on the doors:
'no shirt, no shoes, no service'.
'That's what's public', he says,
'but in private, you can buy
anything you want
if you have the cash'.
He gives her a smug look, like
she's just another Yank who's had
everything handed on a platter.
Does she tell him she was never
the buyer, but the bought?

The band plays country from
'Stand by your Man' to 'Red Neck Woman'.
Before she can speak, he says,
'the thing about women poets,
is they don't think they need to
try to make their poems interesting.
They just expect you to be interested'.
She suspects the only women he'd
find interesting are the ones he could
buy – bodies at his disposal.

UNCLE CHARLIE
In memory of Charles Edward Wright (1935–2017)

At seventeen I stepped off the plane at Newark
wearing homemade churchgoing clothes
and chigger bites from the Quapaw
powwow the night before.
My elegant, ashamed aunt who railed
against the godawful Midwest where they drink
iced tea in winter and overcook their steaks,
whisked me off to Sachs in search
of more suitable clothes –
ivory silk and black chiffon and purple paisley –

but the clothes were worth less to me than
what my Uncle Charlie said when I tried them on.
He brought out the extravagant word 'beautiful'
from the high shelf of his artist's soul,
apparently unaware that nobody wasted
that word on some Ozarks teenager
routinely handed child's menus at restaurants.

He was the first person I met who lived on art,
the first Zen Buddhist,
the first to talk to me like a grown up,
to ask if I'd like a glass of wine,
to go running with me, but only if
we could run slowly enough to
talk about poems and paintings,
which I had never heard a real person do;
it was something that happened only in books,
to people who were nothing like me.

He was my personal guide to Picasso –
from First Communion to the Blind Man's Meal
to Guernica to cubist faces with Iberian eyes,
to line drawings of nudes.

We bought books at the Gotham and Strand,
then stood on a street corner,
a bookstore in one direction,
a Baptist Church in the other.
He turned to me laughing and asked,
'Which will it be? Which will it be?'
By then, a rhetorical question.

Manhattan, KS,
September 12, 2001

A lone bouquet of flowers on the steps of the recently built
    mosque,
Bitter words to hijabed women in the produce section
Lines of uncertainty at gas stations –
midwesterners too busy fearing their own fates
to comprehend those of a city
where people leap from burning towers.
Abdu, the Libyan soccer coach, refs the games
as though it were a night like any other
as leaves turn amber, ember out, at Cico Park.

CLADDAGH RING

'The hands … for friendship,
the heart … for love,
the crown … for loyalty'
– The Claddagh and Celtic Jewelry Company

I have no use for tourist trap legends about it
or guidelines for proper ways to wear it
depending on one's 'relationship status'.

I like the stark, ancient imagery of the crown
resting on the heart – *amor vincent omnia* –
rather than on some over-rated king's head,
and even better, the hands, dexterous and sure,
clasping the heart, so fragile when worn
on a sleeve or exposed to elements.
Whatever life it pulses forward into bliss,
the heart stills without hands to tend to it,
tenderly.

HUMMINGBIRDS
(i.m. Mary McKinley)

Hummingbirds crave the sweetest nectar –
sharply extracting sunlit elixir from
blooms of cochineal, magenta, mauve,
hoping to hoard in fragile bodies
enough to win a night's battle to stay alive,
waking at dawn to begin the frenzied race again.

God was a hummingbird, for Aztecs
who shaped statues from seeds
of purple amaranth melded to honey.
Battle slain warriors reborn as
hummingbirds who fed on the flowers
of the gardens of paradise.

The Mojave tell how, in the beginning,
people living underground in darkness,
sent a hummingbird to look for light.
High above them she guided them up
a twisted path leading to light.

The Ohlone tell how, when the world was near its end,
Hummingbird was sent to the underworld to find fire,
which the Badger people had hidden under deerskin.
Only Hummingbird was small and fast enough
to steal the ember undetected,
burning her throat in the soft whir of her return.

And if her iridescent throat is not enough
to remind us where to find fire,
we have columbine and trumpet vine and bee balm,
morning glory and foxglove and evening primrose,
bleeding heart.

THOMAS DILLON REDSHAW

Thomas Dillon Redshaw describes himself as 'a lapsed poet' who nevertheless has 'on file 2.5 collections ready for any courageous printer'. He is the former editor of *Éire-Ireland* and *New Hibernia Review*. His research focuses on contemporary Irish poetry: he edited *Well Dreams: Essays on John Montague* (Creighton, 2004), and is currently at work on a history of the Dolmen Press. Redshaw writes occasionally for *the Irish Times, The Stinging Fly* and *Poetry Ireland Review*. His collections include *Heimaey*, *The Floating World* and *Mortal*. Redshaw retired from the University of St. Thomas in St. Paul, Minnesota in 2012.

ULLARD STEPS
Tobar Fiachraidh, Cill Ceannaigh

One brown, one white, two mares
Stand off as I walk their churned ground
Up the hill toward the stile.

Three stone steps up, then over,
I put a foot wrong & go down
Like a bag of coal, shoulder first,
Then face down,
                                Silent in the moss
At the edge of the road, the breath
Gone out of me.
                                Deep in that space
Waters slip that fill a stone well below
& hoof prints in their circuit
Where the ground is soft.

WHISTLING A LANDLER,
From Mahler's First

I sit in the intake room waiting for my
Doctor and hers. I sit facing a window,
My left arm reaching out to where
The nurse practitioner had sat taking
My blood pressure, pulse, oxygen level.

I fibbed my way down the check sheet
Of usual questions. Lied about walking
To the nature sanctuary every day. Phonied
Away dawn griefs, the wordlorn laments.
Pointed out antiquated repetitions
In my unrevised bill of medicaments.

Squared up, this morning's sky seems blue.
Polished, new, or clapped-out, all the cars
Parked below line in a diagonal angled
Toward the clean dome of our capital.

SIDE SLEEPER

1

For six years I lay where he lay
All night long on a Boston mattress

Turned to show where his weight
Had rubbed up all that gray

From the silver paint on the spring.
He lay head to the north, barely

Viewing whisps of birch or aspen.
I lay head to the south, seeing into

A barren tangle of spruce branches.
Over his pillow in fading gold

The ghost of a Basket of Plenty
Painted of old on the head board.

Prone and easy there, sharing his rest,
I sometimes woke to find

One chill hand or other
Reaching across the footboard

Into my empty room.

2

These weeks I lie where she lay
All through her late night

In her house, room, red bed
With a tombstone headboard

Old Tom had found for his
First child way back when.

I sleep west with my head
To the footboard. She slept

With her head to the east
Greeting watchers at her bedside.

Then the Passover snowfall.
Then a jar of supermarket tulips

Striped red and yellow, then ...

I sometimes wake from a nap there,
Or from a bad night, only to see

Oak leaves and oak bark
Through the leaded panes

Of her window.

3

I lie on my right. I lie left.
And heave again onto my right.

I lie awake wanting
A welcome at the open door

Of the house of sleep.
Alone on the doorstep,

All through the night.
The landscape of shut-eye

Shows its undreaming
Landmarks. Most easeful

Is that high, indistinct
Horizon between cloud

And field, between more light
And less. Look sharp

And I will see a lantern,
A nervy flick of light

Where we know the
Retina meets the mind.

Following on leads again
To that dark and

Ever-filling well.

FAREWELL

Yes, an old genre scene. The toy train.
The dun freighter off in the cove.

Sons & cousins clustered on the pier.
A gray sunrise. Or a yellow sunset

On a stone jetty reaching into
The calm bay. Daughters & sisters

In red skirts poised on the claddy.
A cow tethered by a risen tide.

The barque still at anchor.
Framed scenes of an old country.

Scenes of a past conjured by loss.
Yes, and by bedside stories

Told back in our heartless land.
In one telling, a curragh. In the other,

A blue lighter. Both heading up
And out, slowly heading still,

Off from here. Yes, in each
The rower's indistinct face grows

Less. Yes, he will take nothing
For his effort. His oars dip, rise,

Sweep back. Her head is shawled,
Her face turned away. White-tipped,

His oars dip, rise, and sweep her
Off away. Dip, rise, and sweep.

ACROSS A LAKE IN ROSEVILLE

Where I had fallen almost conscious

Looking up from the cold sand,
Clear & new ice on the foreshore

At eye-level in this cold, looking
Across the gray & slow waters

Of a lake that would be blue were
I standing where I am lying

Staring over at the far shore, rushes
Brown & papery in November air

That chills the grass up a low bank
To a foundation, to dark windows

Under overhanging eaves & shingles
Of a silent & empty house I cannot enter

Neither awake nor asleep on far ground.

ADRIAN RICE

From Belfast, Northern Ireland, now living with his family in Hickory, North Carolina, Adrian Rice has contributed poetry and prose to *The Belfast Anthology* and *The Ulster Anthology*, both from Blackstaff Press. His latest book is *The Strange Estate: New & Selected Poems 1986-2017* (Press 53, 2018). Previous American titles include *The Clock Tower* (2013) and *Hickory Station* (2015), also published by Press 53. *Hickory Station* was nominated for the Roanoke-Chowan Award for Poetry, and 'Breath' earned a Pushcart Prize nomination. Rice is currently completing Doctoral studies at Appalachian State University, where he teaches in the First Year Seminar Program.

WALLS HAVE EARS
from Eleventh Night *sequence*

Walls have ears. So do the innocent neighbours,
Good neighbours, who have to live with the terrors
That dog their waking and their sleeping, that keep
Them huddled in their house and off their own street.
Evil has manifested itself beside them,
Next door, the kind that knows no sleep, no shame.
      Walls have ears. List'ning to the tale that this wall
Tells from one side of our sectarian sprawl.
A tale told in blood, to the restless music
Of the ceaseless Rave which floods the double-deck
Of the next-door house, commandeered for evil.
The commander-in-chief is a muscle devil.
Here, each rented row is chimney-topped, each row
A funneled Titanic from the shipyard show
That is Harland & Wolff, not more than a stone
Throw away, down the Crum, and across the town.
      Walls have ears. Even the walls would admit to
Fears for the random, chosen civilians who
Will pay the price for their whole population's
Flirtation with freedom. Spilt blood builds nations,
And so does the blood spilt in retribution.
Such tit-for-tat is no lasting solution,
But that's what's being planned in the back kitchen
While the Rave pulses on, lending protection.
      Tonight, the guns will be moved in wheelie bins,
Those plastic Trojans that trundle down back entries
On rubbish removal day …

SPEECH
from Eleventh Night *sequence*

For fuck's sake, has nobody got a pencil?
Are we gonna have to fuckin' cancel
The mural unveiling? Bastards. Someone run
Across the street and ask my oul doll for one.
(And I mean a pencil, ya dirty penis-
Heads. Your dick's off if you mess with my missus.
You'll be a fuckin' eunuch, worse than a fag.)
There's bound to be one in our wee lad's schoolbag.
If there isn't, I'll bloody cane'im maself.
But if there isn't one, check the phone shelf.
    Now, while he's away, are we gettin' ahead
Of ourselves? Can anybody push the lead?
Can anybody fuckin' spell? Properly?
It's the Beeb we're dealing with, not UTV!
Fuck's sake Alfie, you couldn't spell if you were
A fuckin' wizard! Can anybody here
Put two words together for these cam'ra cunts?
The Provies'll say that we all have wee wants
If we don't get our bloody acts together
And write a proper speech. Go get your Heather,
Bobby, she passed the Qualie, didn't she? She's
The woman for the job. She'll be fine. You'll see.
    We can't turn the fuckin' music down, ya dick,
The rave's our fuckin' cover. Are ya just thick?
Apply yourselves here, 'cuz this is important.
In case you've forgotten, I'm your commandant
And if you make me look like a fool, I will
Personally turn you all into pig's swill.
    Now, fuck the Provies and their artsy bullshit,
All those fuckin' fairy murals about shit-
Heads from some culchie past. Fuck'em. Fenian cunts.
They will be the fuckin' ones with the wee wants
If I have my way. Anyway, is Heather
Here yet? If not, big Bobby's in some bother.

OK, here she is now. Good on ye wee girl.
That's a crackin' wee dress there - give us a twirl!
    Now, let's get down to work, we've only an hour
To get this right. When we're done, we'll hit the bar
And watch it on the late night news with a pint
In hand. It'll turn those fenian faces white.
You're askin' me which words we're gonna choose?
I give no fuck. Just make it spell Up The Blues!

CHI

Ritualistically, every night before retiring,
I make sure to close our inside living room slatted-door

which my wife, ritualistically, likes to leave open.
For her, it has something to do with indoor fashion.

For me, the closing has little to do with the flow of chi,
but simply more to do with Belfast me –

a straight run through from you to your rapped front door
in the dead of night was no party.

While I Slept

I was the wick
Unlit at first
As all around me
My birth house
Reassembled itself
From the ground up
Like wax un-melting

Ten or so
The memorable age
Each room reappeared
Each stick of furniture
Showing me what
Had been forgotten
Each family member
Was there

Those now gone
Those still here
And I moved among them
Solid but unseen
I was the wick
Unlit at first
But when everything

Was fully formed
Memory peaked
And I became flame
The house and they
Began to melt away
All that memory
Had rebuilt
While I slept

TOGETHER

I love those nippy cardinals
and their feisty wives,

those lipstick-coloured fusiliers,
flitting through blossomed branches

like children through fields of flowers;
fighting back against big bossy robins

who throw their red-coated
weight around the evening garden.

All glory to the clothed-in-feather!
At least they've learned to live together.

The Frailty of Man
for Malcolm Guite

One night he went sailing tied to a mast in a storm
aged sixty-five, enjoying the frailty of man
The clouds cursed the sea and the sea cursed the clouds
   all night long
on a date with the dark, flirting with fate until dawn

Fear was a
Fear was a
Fear was a
Fear was a friend

Fear was a
Fear was a
Fear was a
Fear was a friend

Fear was a friend and loneliness gave him her hand
they waltzed through the rain that the wind played
   like strings in a band
The ship rose and fell as it curdled its way
   through the foam
he was far from the land but felt he was closer to home

JAMES SILAS ROGERS

James Silas Rogers is a poet and essayist from St. Paul, Minnesota. He is the author of a chapbook, *Sundogs* (Parallel Press, 2006) and a full collection of poems, *The Collector of Shadows* (Brighthorse Books, 2019), and of a mixed-genre book about cemeteries, *Northern Orchards: Places Near the Dead* (North Star Press, 2014). His scholarly writing focuses on Irish-American literature, especially memoir. He was president of ACIS from 2009 to 2011.

SUMMER SONNETS FOR LUCY

He said that he thought that the sonnet ... was the envelope of love, and
if one wanted to write a proper letter to one's love, one had to put it into
a proper envelope.
— John McGahern

FIRST COFFEE

Saturday morning, meeting for coffee
downtown among the urban, oh-so-hip.
We were going to talk about the book
but hardly did. Instead we compared notes
on kids, our careers, and the many hits
we've each taken in our six decades.
(At times we had to halt our conversation,
the espresso machine hissed so loudly.)
Later, walking through the farmers' market,
I asked, *should we go on a proper date?*
and you said *yes* – there amid asparagus
and lettuce, amid the skimpy May crops,
before the summer months would start to bring
the fullness and flavor of green grown things.

Getting to know someone new is like getting
to know an unfamiliar city,
its neighborhoods, parks, arterial streets.
That might be one reason I was pleased
you would ride on public transit with me,
like that night in early June when we caught
the bus for Mears Park at Grand and Grotto
and walked across to a curbside café
on Sixth Street, snagging the only table.
Two grown-ups, out on a Saturday night,
talking at ease over a couple beers,
mapping the shape of our shared connections.
And we both knew, when the check came to us,
the time had come to get back on the bus.

McCarron's Lake

Once again, the way June daylight hangs on
comes as a surprise. After we've paddled
twice around the lake, thinking dark is near,
we head in early, at only 8:00 p.m..
Just for mischief's sake, on our way back
we scatter a flock of resting geese
though by the time we reach shore, they return,
quiet down, and settle in to sleep.

Sunlight lingering, we sit on Pat's deck
sipping drinks and chatting while we let his dog,
Fergus the yellow lab, lick our bare legs.
Summer's arrived like an old promise kept.
Sometimes there are moments that demand
we touch one another. You take my hand.

THE BUTTERFLY HOUSE

Friday afternoon at Como Park Zoo
aimless, casual beauty falls and floats
around us at the Blooming Butterflies,
where insects drift about in a gauzy
quonset hut, random as cottonwood fluff.
Watching them, we cannot help but smile.
How 'incorrigibly plural' it is,
this world that bestows iridescent
wings, streaked, spotted, saturated color,
dancing slowly from flower to flower.
When a butterfly pauses on our arm
we can feel no pressure, detect no weight;
and, still, these resting wings give off a trace
of miracle, as creatures brushed by grace.

CIRCUITS

Ruggles needs his last walk each night at dusk
and I am grateful that many times this year
you've been with me for our nightly routine,
heading out just around the time the day
blends into the dark. On Crocus Hill's streets,
big Victorian homes rest like sphinxes,
watching, just as they've watched generations.
Chimney swifts make trails in the evening sky.
Now and then, fireflies blink on and off.
And we wonder, as we pass these porches,
about the stories behind their windows,
stories still accruing at each address.
Wonder, too, how our story might unfold.

What's summer for, if not for taking walks?
You, me, and the dog continue for blocks.

AMULET

Water halts a fire, but a crumb
of Irish earth from the chapel
of St Mogue-Aidan

that has crossed the ocean
will resist the very strike of tinder.
It can abate the burst

into flashover (the moment
a room's consumed at once
in self-generated flame).

In the meagerest trace
of his clay, a speck that shares
a single atom of electron space

with Wexford's dead saint,
his blessing obtains.
Our safety is sustained.

What is not possible
in such a world as this?
I'll keep and carry a trust in clay.

SÉAMUS SCANLON

Séamus Scanlon is a Galway born writer, librarian and vegan. Books include *The McGowan Trilogy* (Arlen House, 2014), *As Close As You'll Ever Be* (Cairn Press, 2012), *Irlanda en el Carazón* (Artepoetica Press, 2017). Recent output includes *The McGowan Trilogy* production in Japan (www.mcgowantrilogy. com), *The Long Wet Grass* (2018) play production in Ireland by Sellin Players, *The Long Wet Grass* (2017) short film and flash fiction in the Mondays Are Murder slot at Akashic Books. Awards include fellowships from the MacDowell Colony, Dora Maar House, the Center For Fiction (NYC) and a Carnegie Corporation/*New York Times* Librarian Award.

THE LONG WET GRASS

The resonance of tires against the wet road is a mantra
    strong and steady.
The wipers slough rain away in slow rhythmic arcs
    into the surrounding blackness.
The rain falls slow and steady
Reminding me of Galway when I was a child
Where Atlantic winds flung broken fronds of seaweed
    onto the Prom during high tide.
Before the death harmony of Belfast seduced me.

The wind keeps trying to tailgate us.
But we keep sailing.
The slick-black asphalt sings on beneath us.
We slow and turn onto a dirt road, the clean rhythm
    now broken,
high beams tracing tall reeds edging against the road
moving rhythmically back and forth with the wind.
No lights now from oncoming cars.

We stop at a clearing.
I open the door.
The driver looks back at me.
I step out.
The rain on my face is soothing.
The pungent petrol fumes comfort me.
The moon lies hidden behind black heavy clouds.
I unlock the trunk.

You can barely stand from lying curled up for hours.
After a while you can stand straight.
I take the tape from your mouth.
You breathe in the fresh air.
You breathe in the fumes.
You watch me.
You don't beg.

You don't cry.
You are brave.

I hold your arm and lead you away from the roadway,
into a field, away from the car, from the others.
The pistol in my hand pointed at the ground.
I stop.
I kiss your cheek.
I raise the pistol.
I shoot you twice high in the temple.
The coronas of light anoint you.
You fall.
The rain rushes to wipe the blood off.
I fire shots into the air.
The ejected shells skip away.

I walk back to the car and leave you there lying
    in the long wet grass.

A HAON, A DÓ, A TRÍ

I was born and braised in Galway.
Perfect skin
Made in sin.

A Bohermore beauty
From a corrupt mare.

A bastard fair
With sartorial flair.

A blue-eyed stare
Is what I hate with.

I never cry
I never falter
Up the Cathedral marble floor
I slowly saunter
In a fucken halter top
That melts the altar.

Brass, as bold as, my mother vented
Bountiful blood-flow wise I presented
Boot boys bored my fucking head off
Breasts beguiled me in the grey Galway light
Poor Clare bodices on a Sunday night
Blue energy light came through me
And knocked me out.

Bless me sister I am a daughter
I'm Zelda
I don't like fellas like I oughta.

My mother said Zelda you will break my heart
I shoved her down the stairs – she called me a tart.
I clip-clopped down the steps

In my new slip backs
I said – do me a favor Mammy
Die fucken real quick
You lay with a murder man
And now you have me
I'm Zelda
I'll kill ya
A haon, a dó, a trí.

THREE – NIL

High on a Northern Hill
The Golgotha shuffle ended for some.
Fire tried girls
Fetched them in.
I walked in.
The Locomotion was playing.
'Everybody's doin' a brand new dance now'.

They did not see me.
I remember that.
The music played on.

The girls grabbed their bags and ran out the front door.
They pulled it shut after them.
The impact rattled the window panes of the front room.
The boys sobered up – standing up.
Poor boy Brit soldiers.
I shot the three of them once each.
They fell adoration wise.
I remember that.

I shot them each again.
Into their close-cropped teenage skulls
They slouched on the sofa now for good.
They bled away from me.
Next day we drove past the grey wall.
Near the Ligoneill shops.
I crouched low in the back seat.

Teens walked by in parallels and thin bomber jackets
    and skinhead hair cuts
Nonchalantly pointing at the fresh writing for
    photographers.

IRA Three – BRITS Nil

You Are The One

You said it was good luck sign for us
The slick black seals breaking the surface near Nimmo's pier
The rain was falling slow and steady.

The Corrib was in spate carrying all before it.
It was a river of sorrow that flowed through Galway,
Carrying out to sea the limp bodies of
Boys who wanted to be girls of
Girls with ripe pregnant bellies of
Shame and pain tattooed teenagers of
Women fecund with malignancies of
Men that were fighting the wide wings of black angels.
All floating out to Galway Bay and the Atlantic Ocean
All lost forever to black eels and deep channels.

I believed you about the good luck sign.
I threw my Luger far away into the river.

I said – I put some boys into that water.

You turned to me and said
What's done is done.

Victor, you are the one.

IT WAS

It was Galway.
It was a Saturday.
It was 3 pm.
It was a matinee.
Dancing at Lunacy was playing.
It was raining.
It was Galway after all.

The swans at Woodquay were sheltering
behind the granite columns
of the Galway Clifden railway bridge
from the stiff wind coming down from Lough Corrib and
the hard rain coming in from Galway Bay.
The Corrib Princess was tied up against the pier
banging rhythmically against the rubber tire buffers
hanging from the dock's edge.

Two sculls from the Bish were racing for home.
The tall rushes bordering the college grounds swayed and
    bent over heavy with rain.
The bell from the Poor Clare's on Nuns' Island carried
    faintly sadly on the strong breeze.

It was the last time I saw you.

CHARLENE SPEAREN

Charlene Spearen is the Vice President of Academic Affairs at Allen University. She is the Co-founder and director of the university's Langston Hughes Poetry Center. Her credits include a full-length collection of poems titled *A Book of Exquisite Disasters* (University of South Carolina Press, 2012), and a chapbook *Without Possessions* (Stepping Stone Press Editors Series Award, 2006). Her poems have appeared in *Seeking: Poetry and Prose Inspired by the Art of Jonathan Green* (University of South Carolina Press, 2012), *-gape-seed* (Uphook Press, Fall 2011), *Country Dog Review*, as well as other journals. She has facilitated numerous regional poetry workshops.

CATTLE CARS

The coal-cars criss-cross Lake Murray Boulevard, halt
morning traffic and cause the metal rails, miles
of rectangle slats to rumble an alternate reality.
The air bleeds imagination, and the passing cargo
Pushes like the need to turn a page. The steel hum,
now a delicate balance, flips here to there, dismisses
the desire to move. The frame freezes, and I see
bodies hanging to life, eyes dulled, black as a forest's
hollow, bones dressed in rags, and zombie hands,
upturned palms, small ones, so small, whimper and beg.
They coax the next breath, all are, God-forbid,
vertically positioned. Then the cliché: packed in
    like sardines.

WAITING FOR A SIGN

The women inside the train, their faces
a canister of ashes, swing between loss
and the simple wonder if this strange world
would ever come to a stop. Left only with memory
of trees and belief in an omnipotent God,
Katrina, much like a camera's lens, takes in
her child's budding and thinks Mother Nature,
too, is trapped inside a spinning of linear days
that march one, then two, then three.

My God, soon the sign my oldest child is a woman
will come. She wants to tell her daughter they
must jump, run toward the woods faster than the
winter wind's siren. She imagines they are
ballerinas, Russian ballet dancers, and the stage
is waiting. Then a jerk, much like the fox moves
when it spots the unprotected baby rabbit,
the horrendous spinning, metal on metal, slows,
then halts. Spirits coupled with fear and loneliness
turn to hope. The door rolls open. A sea of
    trigger-fingered
guards, all tongues lie still, our eyes, the eyes of
    animals,
do not look right or left, and we breathe
    with our ears.

ALL THAT REMAINS IS THE WIND

Inside a farm house where the moon found
its way through two windows, my baby,
a shimmering reflection of her father,
entered the world. The Gestapo is one
day's march away, but her cry, outrage
marking our mother-daughter journey,
is proof miracles still roam among icicled
cypress trees. At another time I would
have cooed and talked of her, me, us
and how grandiose this whoosh of tiny
life had forever altered the world – would
have spent time with the multiplication:
ten fingers times ten toes. Instead I give
one last push. A force fed by my wish
to strangle the soldier who hovered over
my husband like a hawk with the scent to kill.
The placenta quick on cue passes. I fling
the liver-like flesh, blood dripping between
thumbs and fingers, knowing dark corners
can grow things invisible. I kiss my daughter's
wrinkled forehead, puffed cheeks, tiny fleshy
lips, a dream amongst pure havoc, and swaddle
this precious cargo. The blanket? Bubbee's
star of David stamped shawl, my coat marked
the same. I head into the misty morning
growing power, pain and grief.

SANCTUARY

Under the platform, ignoring the soldier's salacious
talk of the Russian women, I nurse Teteania
for the first and last time. Each suck
fills the tiny belly while my teeth tear at the star's
stitching. Then pulling with need, I crawl
under the first train car; its opened door,
like invitation, offers hope.

A woman with a daughter old enough to care
for a baby sister steps forward. My eyes
plead. Can I do what I must? An act more difficult
than faith. Looking with an amen-stare
at my baby's face, round like the moon that
brought her life, I toss my precious cargo
as if she were garbage wrapped in newspaper,
a bundle now heaved to a Russian mother.

Like the accidental movement
of an artist's pencil, a life-changing
stroke, she caught the reincarnation.
Katrina's baby had only lived three days,
fifty three hours exactly. And like a colonel
rattling a command, she heard this tossed
infant's wail, and the young mother's acid
cry, wide-eyed combustible words gulping
the air like tonic, words running to ignite
the conscience, the fired, 'Let her live'.

BARKING DOGS

Biblical stories are to teach
we are told. The Red Sea parted
to offer safe passage, unheard

of then or now. Faith. Believe
the red door in the next car, chained
from the outside, will open and the God

of Abraham, the Son of Christ will
have mercy. The dogs, an ocean
of curled lips and fangs waited

for the command to tear the transported
prisoner's flesh. I must transcend.
A gift some of the women said.

The young ones, not knowing
the rhythm of a growing womb
the roll of a heel or elbow, the poke

to say I am here, try to coax a rational
plan. At each stop, the routine remained
unchanged, much like grammar or punctuation

rules. We would be fed the thin liquid.
A piece of withered cabbage
floating in a bowl like single leaf

that makes its way to a muddy puddle
And one slice, depending how you define
that word, of stale black bread. Amidst

the crazed barking, the soldiers, guns
pointing, ready to shoot any chosen
target, bark the command: Run

to the woods. Relieve yourself now.
Yet rules have exceptions. The yip
and yap of toss her to fate, no, hide

her formed waves of difference.
Raising my voice, the infant responded
with a wail spurred by protest and hunger.

Survival can fashion anyone into a strange
creature, can twist the story's ending.

DANIEL TOBIN

Daniel Tobin has authored nine books of poems – most recently *From Nothing* (Howe prize); *The Stone in the Air* (after Paul Celan); and *Blood Labors* – and the critical studies *Awake in America*; *Passage to the Center* (on Heaney's poetry); and *On Serious Earth*. Tobin edited *The Book of Irish American Poetry from the Eighteenth Century to the Present*, *Poet's Work, Poet's Play* (with Pimone Triplett), and two collections of Lola Ridge's poetry. Honors include the 'The Discovery/*The Nation* Award', the Penn Warren Award, the Frost Fellowship, the Nason Prize, the Meringoff Award, and the Massachusetts Book Award. He teaches at Emerson College in Boston.

GLENINAGH
An fear gorta ('the hungry grass')

The last stile opens
On lashing wind and rain – a storm
Born on the Atlantic,

Heaving the high moor
Where we walk, bone-soaked and blinkered,
Snooded in our hoods.

We'd followed along
A world's edge, the green road's ledge
From gold strand

To Blackhead, limestone
Like frozen whitecaps in the scutch,
A clean-washed moonscape

Where pavements rise
To ridge and ring-fort, the kestral's
Eyrie of tilt and waft.

Below us, new farms
Leaned fondly into the bay, livestock
Dawdling the verges

Marking drystone walls
Of remnant fields, beside them buried
In hawthorn and hazel

The hovels of the lost,
The starving lying where they fell, heaved
Into mass graves, the rest

Shipped out, others
Hunkered, scratching it out: the few, fittest,
Or were they the fiercest?

On this wide saddle
Between two terraced mountains, high above
That tower house staring

Blankly at the waves,
We bow our heads toward un-hungry grass,
Eying the way marks,

And bowing lower still
To side-blowing wind, side-blown rain – this
Light touch of the merciless.

AN ERRATIC

The way the ice
plucked it flatly out of bedrock
for a slow dance across the moraine, all
thrust and surge behind its forward raft along
the lens, an outlay of till and spalling underneath,
hashes of Pleistocene sediment over slabs and floes,
no holdfasts in the lodgments, these as-if infinite ablations
where the pavements – all fractured klint and grike – mimic
outwash where the glacier like a flagrant tongue licked along
the planet's slowly gouged and polished ridge depositing seed
in slim fissures lately equatorial give or take a hundred eons,
and others smaller, less impressive in the meltwater channels
away from shore, forming trains of boulder fields, frozen
ruckus of stone allied to stone, and all of them outcasts
in the riven historical shambles the legends once held
were evidence of some shared ancient deluge, Biblical,
Sumerian, Mayan, Olmec, when the Sun blotted
out, or God or gods grew petulant
with the failings of the wandered
world,
so what moves
now must stay balancing
impossibly where Earth before it spreads its lone horizon
to the sky ...

THE SIXTIES
after Aidan Rooney's 'The Seventies'
and Mary O'Donoghue's 'The Eighties'

Incinerator dreams, the garbage bagged and thrown.
Why does the Cue Ball Man want to bury us?
A gray-coated boy salutes his father underground.
Missile crisis. Duck and Cover. Sacred Heart bless.

Across the foreign cross a dead man walks barefoot.
O cigarette fogged kitchen! O boiling meat pot!
Who speaks the microwave's susurrus of stars *en route*?
Ouija board. Spin-the-bottle. Kill-count *tete a tete*.

How did the TV turn from black and white to color?
Crayola radiator. Napalm GI-Joe.
Earthrise. Stickball chalk dust. The acronym murders
Cram streets until they bleed. Black out. *To boldly go…*

One small step by man, one giant leap above the air.
Screech anthems thrill the naked tribes. Me not there.

THE VACATION

After all the forethought
still it felt so far away,
the months like years,
weeks like months, days
of frenzied preparation,
work quietly laid aside,

and urgent hours before
the uplift of departing,
grateful even for queues,
all the harried weight
of going, each moment
quickened to this single
second.
          How indelible
our disappearance,
a monument to time
elapsed and saved –
limestone ridges, sky,
a white-tailed eagle
soaring out of sight.

WITH THE GIFT OF A FEATHER AT COOLE PARK

Nothing left of the great house now
But these stuttering steps
Leading nowhere,
A tearoom selling crepes,
Day-trippers with their camera-ready phones
Vaguely on the hunt for swans.

We walk again these sodden woodland trails
Enwound like loosened twine,
Attending viewpoints of the famed reserve.
Fields away, the M18
Gouges its karstic scar to new estates
Where the ranging city starts.

Years ago, the prospect of these woods
(or was it just our wants)
Quickened us. The tracts of felled or fallen trees
Spurred by rot, acid rains,
Offer vantage onto lowland rills
Before those fossil hills.

At the lakeshore where the turlough floods,
A son – his father turned
Aside to some distance in his mood
He holds apart – skips stones
Ardently into the still waters
And the gray wash glumly stirs.

I would teach him how to choose the one,
Judge its shape, its feel
Along the angled finger and the palm,
To see the sightline clear
Until along a mirror's windless sky
It skipped to his wide eye

The arrowed ripples spreading on the brim.
We turn away instead
To find in scrabble this one feather,
The bird flown from its shed.
It could be a child's quill, pure white.
At the frill the faintest brush of night.

DAVID RAY VANCE

David Ray Vance is the author of two award-winning collections of poetry: *Vitreous* (Del Sol Press, 2007) and *Stupor* (Elixir Press, 2014). His poems and stories have appeared in such journals as *Chicago Review, Denver Quarterly, Notre Dame Review* and *McSweeney's.* He is Creative Writing Program Director at the University of Texas at San Antonio and the recipient of a University of Texas System Regents' Outstanding Teaching Award. He is also editor of *American Letters & Commentary,* which after 20+ years as an annual journal of literature and art has transitioned into a book press dedicated to experimental writing.

Pregnant Pause in Spring

Male wood bees, while aggressive
compared to their female counterparts
lack stingers.

This I learn in passing conversation.
Somewhere close by a hive,
inside it a murder of multifaceted
eye machines, wings & antennae.

I picture the tumors in my head
yet to be diagnosed, how like cataracts
they will manifest occlusion.

Fecund buzz of mitosis blooming
purple on my mind's Nile-like deltas.

And in frustration admonish Milton
(again in passing) his garden a workaday
paradise, clocked in/clocked out.

Whatever the fear engendered
or engineered, what we most desire
most urgently, is Eve's grave awareness
that sting of self-recognition.

The tragic demands we bare ourselves
or else suffering presents
as symptom rather than disease.

When I squint the sun but momentarily
I am dizzy the whole day after.

As though my eyes were being pried
from inside, as if dilator muscles
were frozen open.

Always there is a pattern to discern
whether you impose it yourself
is (probably) beside the point, barbed
or smooth, venomous or benign.

Male bees, I'm told, are called drones
and their tongues are defectively short
so they cannot feed themselves.

Every fall, the females, called workers
stop feeding them, drag them
from the hive, and leave them to die.

After the fall, they are regenerated
by the one, sovereign queen.

NORTH PACIFIC GYRE

The earth moves but these waters
are a dead eye.

We travel under our own power.
No wind. Hardly a wave.

Not through pristine blue
but amidst a multicolored mosaic

of bottles, bottle caps, wrappers,
and plastic fragments.

A literal sea of shoes, hockey sticks,
rubber ducks, you name it

webbed together with mono-
filament fishing line

and tangles of nylon netting.

Each object a relic of human
intention, every strand of polymer

desired, demanded, capitalized
into existence.

You and I did that. You and I
at the grocery store

inside the box retailer
our ideals, our lack of them

double-packaged and shrink-
wrapped for freshness.

Not waste, but wasted.
Or else how?

Nevermind the outgassing.
We pay in cash.

Or irony upon irony,
put it on our plastic.

In [Medias] Res

i. *Begins [sadly]*

With the greatest pomp
but moderate circumstance.
In a mirrored hall backed
with lilac crepe streamers.
After the bride throws
her bouquet. The sun again
in everyone's eyes. Dusky
swallows crowd diving,
coveting hair. A depraved
glance between two strangers
at a chance intersection.
Heat waves atop hot metal.
Six egg-shaped stones
rattling a pocket.

ii. *Continues [self-consciously]*

In descriptions overwrought
and supercilious. Punctuated
with extravagant feigned laughter.
Hands in beards fishing table
scraps. A winter's worth of wood
'laid in', as the cutters say
rubbing their knuckles for heat.
Table laden with cheap tchotchkes.
While the neighborhood dogs
dodge the usual questions:
Do you fret the instrument thus?   ·
Must worry portend or preclude?
When the past transpires what then
shall we breathe?

iii. *Ends [audibly]*

No flowers or sweet confetti
or ticker tape cascade.
The starter's pistol still warm
in its zippered case. Ire blank
as a blood chit where train
tracks meet horizon.
Before the mad conductor
punches your ticket
with his fang-like baton.
The band having abandoned
the written score long before
any icebergs appear.
Every last damsel fly untied.
Eyes blind, moon-winked.

DRUCILLA WALL

Drucilla Wall has authored *The Geese at the Gate* (Salmon, 2011) and *The Irish Summers* (Salmon, forthcoming), and has co-edited the collection *Thinking Continental: Essays and Poems of Place* (Nebraska, 2017). Her poems and essays appear in various literary and scholarly journals, and are anthologized in *Red Lamp Black Piano: The Caca Milis Cabaret Anthology*; *The People Who Stayed: Southeastern Indian Writing After Removal*; and *True West: Authenticity and the American West*. She teaches American and Native American Literatures; and Essay and Poetry Writing at the University of Missouri-St. Louis. Her Ph.D in English is from the University of Nebraska.

WATERSHED WARNING

Erect blue towers on my body;
I lie low in sweet reflection,
to all my creatures give provision;
I layer the stone to mark the way.

At my edges leave your boot print;
test my wetlands with your poisons,
where the absent salamanders
follow with me to the river.

Light of weasel, light of vole,
light of eagle, trout, and otter –
all my wild geese sound the trumpet.
Regard your mother.
I will take you down

Burren Wall

In summer the cattle graze the high patches made rich on
    limestone
leaching into thin topsoil, rain generally arriving or about
    to arrive.

In winter they shelter in the lower fields, upper and lower
    segmented by vast
acres of bald grey stone paving hills and running to the
    turloughs and the shore.

Loose rocks common, we struggle to follow the young
    farmer's pace to the top.
His voice elevates over wind, naming plants, telling the
    stories of his family's land.

A Famine wall shoots a straight useless line across the
    highest slope over a bed
of bare slab, the end burrowing into mist. I am the only
    one to see their eyes.

Who will be fed? Who is deserving? Who has earned the
    soup? Who has got
the passage, and who is lifting stones in fever? Who is
    buried on the Atlantic

on their way to Gross Isle? Which ancestor pays for a
    ranch on the bitter
Montana prairie, his dollars bought with bones? The best
    are never survivors.

We pick our way down, knees straining, making note of
    wild thyme, oxeye daisy,
rockrose, heather, and gorse, with the bloody cranesbill
    blanketing all open ground

WILD ORCHIDS

That was the year we strode the prom
between the rail line and the Slaney River,
turning under the bridge to climb back
to the rush of traffic on the road to town.

Massed in the field that was your boyhood
soccer pitch, wild orchids towered
over us, swaying above the ferns and grasses,
their purple blooms drifting like faces
brightened in the sunlit mist, witness
to the river, passing trains, the lone blue heron,
horses on the island, and our rain-jacketed selves
complaining of the weather and wondering
how to solve this or that, here or there.

One time we saw a double rainbow arc
the river on the tide's retreat to Wexford.
From a chestnut tree a nightingale pierced
the summer night with its lament,
and we knew none of our cynical friends
would believe such walks real or even possible.

Progress pocked the town.
Some nights a smell of burning threaded
all along the streets like a builder's promise.
Yellow machines scraped the ground raw
of rubble behind the market square
where the old hotel once stood.
Across the street a new Dunnes Stores
stretched tall as the cathedral,
and the *Irish Times* announced to all
that orchids were in trouble.

Our last night on the river path we paused
by bog cotton, and wild flowers
to watch fish jump and hope
for no further improvements.

SEA CLIFF VIEW, SOUTH WEXFORD

You must be going fishing
somewhere farther down the beach.
Why else carry the awkward case
bumping your thigh
with each failing footprint
in the rolling pebbles that breathe
with each wave's retreat?

Maybe the rod rests in your other hand
just beyond my sight,
blending with the frothed rollers
that tumble under the rising wind.
It might be a patch of mackerel
surfacing by the dark rocks.
The tide slants away in evening
hesitation before folding below
the breakers to thrust all it can carry
out into the channel.

Let that be a tackle box you heft
into the surf. Let there be
a strong-shouldered sandbar
a little ways out that offers
the best chances. Let it be only
my weak eyes losing sight
of you beneath white horses.

FUSHIMI-INARI-TAISHA

Twin Fox-dogs in scarlet neckerchiefs
companion the dead at shrines
punctuating ease of cedar and bamboo
groves along the mountain path,
remainders of human pain.
Ten thousand shrines, two stone dogs for every
soul swirling in the mottled shade.
Early violets tilt sunward
in the breaks beside knockings
high among bamboo trunks,
a lonely crow complaining.
Turn and return to ten thousand
scarlet torii gates and hundreds
taking the good luck path this Wednesday
in Kyoto on the lower slopes.
Ring the temple bells for good fortune.

On a corner past the venders' stalls,
among small shops and restaurants,
five cats wait at the Neko Café,
a place where you can go to play
with cats and pay for your time.
They blink your way at the door
in perfect balance with the golden afternoon,
one paw extended from a chair or windowsill.
The Neko Café is a cat café.
The tabby presents his belly to your hand:
'Pilgrim', he says, 'Less self, more God'.

EAMONN WALL

Eamonn Wall has authored seven books of poetry, most recently *Junction City: New and Selected Poems 1990-2015*. Essay collections include *From Oven Lane to Sun Prairie: In Search of Irish America, Writing the Irish West: Ecologies and Traditions,* and *From the Sin-é Café to the Black Hills: Notes on the New Irish,* winner of the Durkan Prize from ACIS. With Saeko Yoshikawa, he co-edited *Coleridge and Contemplation.* A Co. Wexford native, Wall serves as Professor of International Studies and English at the University of Missouri-St. Louis. He is a past-president of ACIS and a vice-president of Irish American Writers & Artists Inc.

Hungry for flight our tricolor
takes air before morning's first rays
have roused the castle's cobblestones
or pushed deep into shaded lots –
like garter snakes unwinding out
from deep grasses and dark crevasses.

All night I had dreamed of you
touched those tender knots
behind your knees, kissed vagrant
signposts that line your back
pole to pole, track to track.

Sunny with some slight cloud cover
a wildish wind comes and goes
as a rebel prodigal who might raise
for Michael Collins and Wolfe Tone
a villanelle against the epic of the state.

At a long table in the Silk Road Café
two young men sit quietly holding hands.
Let freedom ring is the slow air of their display.

OLEANDER

Petals of red oleander are pinned to stems
as airfoil blades are to propellers shaped.

White oleander opens as a handshake should
on a red leaf path leading inland to your town.

Oleander is the flower of Hiroshima,
kyochikuto first to rise in bloom after the city
had been bombed by Enola Gay, many

observing along pathway and hillside
hopeful oleander red, then oleander white

sharp as uniforms of nurses who wandered ward
to ward, cafeteria to parking lot, to tented homes.

I walk through the Show-Me-State
with Roscoe Jones to whom the oleander
is lethal. Where the park's perimeter greets
the Osage Trail, he pauses a moment
moving homeward. These Missouri oleanders
that climb a wooden fence nearby
are *nerium oleander, laurel de jardin,*
rosa Francesca, jia zhu tao, dogbane, in Irish
oiliander, and thought by cranks to offer a cure
for cancer. Roscoe pauses another moment
to account for me, to register how
to one another we are linked, to affirm
my current space on his turning wheel,
the manner of my gait, and what measure
he can gauge of my Monday disposition.

Across sub-divisions, on far-off hills the sublime
is wise and liquid red and white written for Hiroshima.

RED WINGED BLACKBIRDS

Today through field glasses
I observe one small flock
of red-winged blackbirds
busy about the Audubon
Center, the viewer narrowing
space to a single frame
while dreadlock lines crossing
over top whir rhythm sweet
as monks might chant compline.

Seed has been rattled to earth,
grasses through lens magnified.

Of wind, grass and bird sound
no hard register rebounds indoors
though as song I intuit warbling
ear to ear, sweet as a lover's purr.

Nowhere guns, booty, murder,
mayhem, not even the whizz
cut of an automobile.

Like my
grandmother, the red-winged
blackbirds do no harm. We sit
in the 1960s side-by-side
at the kitchen table drinking tea
afternoon running along
as its own great fearless river.

At my back
today, two miles away, things
merge together – confluence
of the Missouri and Mississippi

Rivers, red-winged blackbirds
returning to the frame to feed.

Grandmother taught me to be
for silence watchful and how
to merge with it, then float away.

Under the crucifix was where he'd been seated
though given no succor by dead-on-the-wall.
Without a pinch of ambition, no clue what to do,
she found nothing of interest in thick Tony Small.
So he sat very still, the cat had his tongue,
sigh of the counselor did mean he was stupid,
empowerment of youth by then not invented.

Bob Dylan his confessor preached always resist
though he owned no phrase his counselor to twist.
Young and dismayed, the width of a flea, he could
hardly deflect her ring of authority to mere tap
on the wrist. One thin slice of life is what we are
granted: wise books passed along it's often
too late; school's train left the station, quarter-to-eight.

GRANDMOTHER: AFTER SCHOOL

the best teacher lives outside, the best teacher lives inside you,
beating blood, breathing air, the best teacher is alive.
– Joanne Kyger

Buttered toast flavored with raspberry
preserve grandmother prepares for me.
Annie Murphy pours two cups of tea,
seats herself across the table, the kitchen
of the old house on Barrack St. warm,
its exterior walls thick as tractor tires
where, settling, she hears each loosened
episode of a boy's day at school, her
gaze a poultice to draw out a wound
or to reveal passage to a brighter room,
her dark blue dress marked by a starched
white linen collar, her faint gazes and soft
gestures abate the wind that makes
all children crazy, as mother likes to say,
her eyes call to mind season's sunny days,
summer time and ease, old and kinder ways.

When grandmother came to live with us,
mother told me once, she brought
but one small suitcase, all her adult life
having inhabited one guest room at the hotel
she had opened, that granny liked to add
how confined space allowed for certain
freedoms to emerge, not to own or be
submerged in many accessories, shoes,
and clothes. I recall still her elegance
of dress, how always her face and hands
sparkled with cleanliness. Her husband,
a most contrary man, fitted his possessions
into twin containers: a worn brown valise
and shiny shaving bag to join our rowdy band:
visitors all traversing a green and fertile land.

Today, rain beats the thick plate glass
of the high-rise where from my desk
I sweep cups-to-go and bagels by forced air
desiccated into a metal bin, growing
more aware, root or rhizome, of hobnailed
bosses who think all female wisdom willful
cut wafer thin. She favored all shades
of blue, her dark shoes polished into light,
her hair like a girl's caught by a bright barrette.
We savored an hour together at the kitchen
table sharing tea, school dusting off, Annie
Murphy – I called her Granny Annie – and me.

LAWRENCE WELSH

An award-winning journalist and essayist, Lawrence Welsh has published 12 books of poetry, including *Begging for Vultures: New and Selected Poems, 1994–2009* (University of New Mexico Press). This collection won the New Mexico-Arizona Book Award. It was also named a Notable Book by Southwest Books of the Year and a shortlist finalist for both the PEN Southwest Book Award and the Writers' League of Texas Book Award. Born and raised in South Central Los Angeles, Welsh lives in El Paso, Texas. His selections for the anthology come from his manuscript *A Hoolie for the Yanks*.

HOGAN

close to 'refinery'
i found the truck
or trucker
saying 'hogan'
and then 'drive for hogan'
in st. louis
missouri

i inspected
flat firestones
the bracken
reaching
the shotgun side

hogan
i thought
a family name
my family name
of chieftains
and tipperary kings

the ones lost
like out of state
drivers
stranded on a new road
looking for the familiar
the ones they've known
as home

SWAN'S RUIN

blacked out
mississippi
malt liquor
or *guinness*
here
is good for you

that
i believe
but 360s
over and over
with white feathers
scattered
on lough derg
dromineer
and his stagger
to shore
mumbling: *cure cure*
or a way
simply back
to the water

After Hartnett, After Kavanagh

whiskey in jest
like tasting full glasses of jamesons
or is it paddy's march
to powers gold label?

such privilege taken away
but restored in not touching
for a ticket to live
a chance for survival under the fumes
the never reaching out
with a skeleton hand
the cries from a barren bog
the 'set 'em up lad we'll top it off again'

and the remembrance of destruction
like where'd i leave my bike
and who stole my horse?

it's in the flowers
in the air
in the creature's promise to forget it
you won't need it at all

so call its name again
and remember the blackness and forgetting
it's part of its special charm
known for its fleeting cure

THE HIDE OFF

lawnmower
was stash too:
    old crow's bed
for shaking hands
when my mother said:
    'pity the bottles
        everywhere'

pity maybe
    paints
hope of who
    knows
the juice delivers clicks
known and
unknown
like fists or razors
or river shannon's promise
of blarney
    stone:

o billy barry friendships
were smoke and liquor
the tin sign – all four feet high:

      'paddy whiskey'

but that was
world war two
and any bowler hat of
green moss
we
    send up
      salutes
machinations for them all

back home my
mother shook her head:

'go find the bottle son
i could use a belt myself'

New Hibernia

ballycommon
as spinner
to lough derg
shannonvale
where we part
lace curtains
for all
honeymoons home
they say

and coolaholiga
dissected and spliced
burnt and thrown out
like old thatch
on the new dublin road

wait, i say
to my children
your time is coming
like mine
first at 16
to the vacant
ormond hotel
o'shea's encampment
at portroe
and the stumbling home
half beaten
half drunk
from nenagh town

then the new
as old
the remembrance
of collapse
of rising

the closing off
of the circle again

and then for them
a digging
to the old world
to the new
and a place
their place
like mine
somewhere
in between

ACKNOWLEDGEMENTS

The editor gratefully acknowledges the support of the ACIS Executive Committee chaired by its President, Timothy G. McMahon; the superlative advice of the ACIS poets, most particularly Christine Casson, Kathryn Kirkpatrick, David Lloyd, Ed Madden, Daniel Tobin, Drucilla Wall and Eamonn Wall; and the indefatigable efforts of the publisher, Alan Hayes of Arlen House. We also thank Randall Exon and Logan Grider for permission to reproduce their art works. Exon's painting 'The Tourist' is in the collection of Robin Wagner-Pacifici and Maurizio Pacifici.

.

*

Eamonn Wall has been my closest companion in this endeavor, encouraging me when the project seemed unworkable, informing me when I was hampered by limited expertise, chivvying me when other responsibilities delayed me, advising me when I was uncertain, heartening me when I felt overwhelmed. This anthology is infinitely the better for his unwavering enthusiasm.

Alan Hayes has sustained this project with intelligence and determination, and I greatly appreciate his firm direction, his brisk efficiency and above all his confidence in the work. The poets included in *Open-Eyed, Full-Throated* are grateful beyond words for his support.